"This is a good book. It is a book that men will read and enjoy. Chocolate or Lunch takes a lot of the guess-work and stress out of being in relationship. I was surprised at how much conflict that I normally brought into my relationships. This book taught me a better way. The blessing at the end of the book is spectacular."

-- **Chuck Pettet**, Commodities Trader

"With simple, clear examples and exercises, Chocolate or Lunch delivers a powerful message: the choices we make and attitudes we hold define the quality of our relationships and our own happiness. The authors' gentle guidance supports the reader in making a transformative journey through their own thoughts, feelings, and experiences to discover a new, more fulfilling way of being."

-- **C.J. Hayden**, Author of 50 Ways Coaches Can Change the World

"Chocolate or Lunch is full of tools about how the human mind and heart work in harmony. This is a book about relationships that prompts you to go back and read it over and over as you navigate through the text and discover meanings and lessons that apply.

I found the stories powerful and helpful looking for lessons that I could take away. The language is easy to read and yet powerful. I can easily see myself keeping it at close proximity so I can go to it when relationships and feelings get out of whack and I need to recalibrate."

-- **George Theotocatos**, Retired Oil Company Executive

"The stories, the important quotes from insightful and evolved individuals, and the beautiful conclusions and very helpful questions all combine to make a truly useful tool for individual and collective progress. Our relationships have been so tainted by our understanding of our experiences. Your book helps to put our experiences into right perspective and focus us on more positive and productive thinking. Our thoughts definitely become our actions."

-- **Kathy Penn**, Montessori Teacher

"I found a lot of thoughtful suggestions to ponder. My heartiest kudos to you both for 'just doing it!' Less talk, more action -- always a good thing."

-- **Janice Auth**, Author/editor of *To Beijing and Beyond: Pittsburgh and the United Nations 4th World Conference on Women*

"I'm excited about this uplifting and valuable book, filled with fresh insights for new seekers and old. Although most of the concepts were familiar to me, fresh perspectives gushed forth as I read. The conversational tone feels like a visit with friends. Bravely authentic personal examples bring the content to life. Buy an extra copy as a gift."

-- **Sharon Lippincott**, Author of *Adventures of a Chilehead*

"Taking time to be positive, what a difference! Book looks awesome. Very pertinent and great timing! Loved the story about the daughter asking what happened in the mother's day. The three things that make you happy rule, what a great and easy way to stay positive and focused on the 'right' things."

-- **Mark Curry**, MacFarlane Group

"*I feel blessed to have been asked to edit* Chocolate or Lunch: How Choices Impact Relationships. *While doing so, I was able to immediately apply the wisdom within to shift some troublesome dynamics in my current relationship. I intend to read and study this delightful volume again and again, as there is much to be gained by doing so.*"

-- **Joyce B. Wilde, M.S.**, Author of *The Wilde Woman's Guide to Organizing in Five Simple Steps: Using Mindfulness to Change Your Habits*

"Chocolate or Lunch *is well written, simple enough for anyone to gain helpful approaches to the major inner issues that we all encounter. The writing style is warm and inviting so that readers can easily absorb and contemplate what is being treated. The exercises are helpful and offer genuine guidance. It is a gift of a book.*"

-- **Hugh Leonard**, Author of *Interiority Powered*, Executive Coach

"*Love the stories!!! They help to put flesh on the bones of your insights!! Thanks for sharing!*"

-- **Sister Maureen Fitzgerald, ascj**, Principal at St. Rita School

"*We can be happy. We can be at peace. That is what we all want and that is the message Nancy Smyth & Sharon Eakes deliver with profound wisdom and heartfelt grace. Relationships are at the core of life and Nancy and Sharon guide us through how we can shift our internal choices to enjoy deeper more satisfying relationships, at work and at home. A lyrical, lovely read with lasting impact!*"

-- **Kelly Epperson**, Book Coach, Author of 25+ Books, Erma Bombeck essay contest judge

CHOCOLATE OR LUNCH
How Choices Impact Relationships

Cover Art: Nancy Smyth
Cover Design: Suzanne Oviedo

www.chocolateorlunch.com
www.twowisewomen.org

beinspired@twowisewomen.org

ISBN 978-0-578-15568-5

Printed in USA

CHOCOLATE OR LUNCH

How Choices Impact Relationships

Nancy Smyth and Sharon Eakes

Contents

GRATITUDE

NANCY: I am grateful for the abundant blessings I have received. Quite particularly, I'm thankful that sacredness and meditation have been an integral thread throughout my life. I bow with respect and love to my meditation master, who inspires me to ever expand.

I offer my endless gratitude to my family who has always truly known, loved and supported me. Thank you, as well, to all my friends; I treasure you and your beautiful hearts. I am especially grateful to Chuck Pettet, our dedicated reviewer, and Noelle Matzek, a brilliant and most valuable assistant. I can ask either of them anything and they respond, always wholeheartedly. Both have contributed their hearts as well as their wisdom. They stood so very close to me that sometimes we shared the same shoes. My heart fills with thanks for you.

I thank my colleague and co-writer, Sharon Eakes. Sharon is amazing. She is as brilliant as a benevolent shining star, generously adding her warmth, her joy, her light to every collaborative project we launch. She imbues our work with effervescent possibilities, making it always fun, creative, and most significantly, a sacred adventure. In the development of this book, she astutely translates our hearts' messages into words with clarity. What a prize it is to have such a colleague. I celebrate our co-authorship. My prayer is that our book can satisfy the hunger of people that truly want to know how to live peaceful, happy lives.

SHARON: I have abiding gratitude for my parents, Leon and Weedie Eakes, who modeled loving for me in a remarkable way for 60+ years. What a gift! I am profoundly thankful to Bahá'u'lláh, founder of the Bahá'í Faith, and to my vibrant Pittsburgh Bahá'í community for continued guidance, inspiration and support. To my family, especially my children Lisa and Gordon Mitchell, thank you for encouraging me every step of the way. My friends hold me up. In the writing of this book I have especially been helped by Astrid Kersten, Stephanie Parrott, Dona Luedde and Sallie Davis.

Collaborating in writing a book presents many opportunities to practice heart-centered relating, as the authors navigate their way to finding one voice. I have especially valued Nancy Smyth's wisdom, graciousness, humor, and poetic soul. The beautiful poetry included in the book comes from that soul! I also want to acknowledge Nancy's loving persistence and discipline. She kept us on track. Nancy and I share a deep desire for all people to experience open-hearted, productive, rewarding relationships. That desire comes from the core of each of us. Sometimes while we were doing our glorious collaborative dance across the miles, the strength of that desire was so great, we could almost feel the phone wires sizzle. I am grateful for that experience!

TOGETHER: Our appreciation goes to Kelly Epperson, author and mentor, for encouraging us to trust, and write what we know wants to be written, to Joyce Wilde, our constructive and caring editor, to Siobhan McDonald for her generous editing of the poems, and to Suzanne Oviedo who enthusiastically designed the exciting cover and turned a Word document into a beautiful book. Heartfelt thanks also to Sharon Lippincott for her careful reading and valuable feedback.

May our book honor all the great philosophers, sages, teachers and authors who have been dedicated to the pursuit of truth and generously share it with us. We are grateful to The Arbinger Institute for providing the forum where we met and started down the path of exploring relationships in new ways. Their faith in us encouraged an ever-deeper journey.

Our hearts graciously thank each and every client for trusting us and bravely doing what is necessary to transform struggles into healed relationships. You have been great exemplars of courage and peace. We have fallen in love with each of you; it has been a privilege to be on your journey with you.

A special round of applause goes to each of you, who willingly offered your story. You have made this book possible. Every share is full of wisdom and inspiration, leaving much for readers to ponder in order to evolve and tell their own stories. Thank you.

Our most heartfelt thanks to everyone in our lives who has been patient with us and helped expand our capacity to love. You have offered us the ticket to happiness.

INTRODUCTION

Critical mother? Difficult boss? Disrespectful teenager? Uncaring spouse? Oh, no!

We truly hope not. Instead, we wish you fulfilling and satisfying relationships. However, if you have even *one* tense relationship and you've tried everything you can think of, and nothing has changed -- this book is for you. We'll help you see what has been in the way of solving the difficulties in relationships and outline a dependable path to follow. You can think about it as a stable foundation that will provide you with the best life possible.

If you are anything like us, you want to enjoy the people in your life, the work you do and the beauty and varied experiences in this world. The moments of life are delicious and meant to be enjoyed, even savored. Sometimes we stray from this joyful perspective. Many things can get us off track: beliefs, obligations, feeling stuck and being upset. How tragic it is to lose out on the precious relationships and treasured moments of our lives. There is no need to do that at all. We know that for a fact.

As facilitators and professional coaches, relationships have been the focus of our work. We have also personally applied what we are sharing. It works; we live happy lives and are excited to share our experience with you.

To our utter delight, people we work with throughout the world have been able to amend what felt like impossible relationships. We've watched near miracles as they resolved struggles that seemed doomed to remain intractable.

1

We and our clients have shifted in ways that are much deeper than behavioral -- far beyond changing words or acting differently. These shifts require an honest look into the heart of matters. And when a difficult relationship changes, it feels as if our entire world -- internal and external -- expands and becomes brighter.

Our major premise is that limited perceptions, the very way we see and think, are the cause of unhappiness in relationships. When we learn to see with our hearts, we find happiness, and suffering dissolves. What a free and satisfying life that creates!

The ideas in this book are radically different from mainstream ways of thinking about relationships. In order for them to be absorbed, we introduce them from many different angles. We'll suggest exercises and give you questions to ponder to rejuvenate your relationships. These practices will help you assimilate the concepts and create more understanding.

Throughout the book, we'll focus on how we *see*, what we *think*, how we *feel*, and what we *do*. This approach takes us on an inner journey to see and know ourselves in ways that may be surprising. To encourage your ongoing resolve, we've provided true stories from our own missteps and our clients' breakthroughs. (Oftentimes client names have been changed to maintain privacy.) The stories are offered to be both instructive and inspiring.

A sincere inner journey moves our hearts naturally to an outer journey. With increased awareness and understanding comes humility; we begin to see people with new eyes. This openness allows our hearts to be touched by others' hearts. We discover people in a completely new light. What we previously thought was true falls away and frees us up to genuinely love, no longer burdened by feelings from constricted thoughts. That shift in perception is helpful in all our relationships, including those with family, friends, and coworkers.

A happy heart is as real as the ground we walk on.

Courageously try on everything offered here to determine what works for you, even if it feels awkward at first. Take a leap of faith about what is possible in all of your relationships. Reading this book will give you some value and may be engaging. However, a better life will result by plunging wholeheartedly into the work contained here. *Chocolate or Lunch* raises deeply thoughtful considerations -- go slowly, answer questions, see what occurs, and make changes.

Everything we discuss in this book takes practice, building strong muscles of compassion, patience, and perhaps forgiveness as well. It is possible to mature and expand both our mind and heart for such an Olympian task. Walk step by step through the chapters as if you were preparing for an auspicious event. This book will get you there, one concept, one exercise, and one story at a time.

We'll begin looking at your desire for happiness and carefully map out the way to get there: from embracing the wonder of your heart and mind, to learning how to merge them together in order to resolve problems, and set you free. The journey we are on in relationships will open us to more love inside than we have imagined possible. On the journey, we shift from wanting happiness to being happiness.

We will walk with you every step of the way.

You'll find a helpful Study Guide at the end of the book. We've designed this for either individual or group study. It can be used chapter by chapter as you move through the book, helping you digest each chapter. Or it can serve as a way to continue the journey after completing the book.

Sustainable change takes time, practice, and nurturance that only you can give it. We guarantee great benefits from pausing, pondering, and practicing. We also invite you to be alive to what unfolds in your heart, contemplating its meaning and putting its wisdom into action.

We warmly welcome you and are delighted that you are joining us.

HAPPY

Step Closer to People

Happy at home. Happy at work. Happy! An auspicious undertaking; how do we get there?

Let's begin with stories from each of us.

> NANCY: *When my daughter, Anita, was 16, I would come home from work tired, fearful and even angry. I'd drag myself through the door, grouchy as all get out. Each day like a sacred ceremony, Anita would simply ask in a loving tone, "Tell me three things that happened today that made you happy."*
>
> *I'd grumble and snarl. She would kindly repeat, "Tell me three things that happened today that made you happy." I worked hard to find one and I would blurt it out like a train engineer shouting, "All aboard." I felt so done with this game and stamped my foot to get my own way.*
>
> *Anita would say, "Good, two more."*
>
> *Every day we would do this routine 'til I could produce three things that made me happy that day and then, SURPRISE, I was happy.*

What made Nancy happy? Is it magic?

In a way it is. She embraced a magic that is inside all of us. It's a subtle magic, inherently ours and so profound that it sometimes eludes us.

SHARON: *It was a snowy evening and I was on my way home from work, a little frazzled. A bridge was out, so I had to drive extra miles, and I'd forgotten to defrost food for dinner for my kids and me. Most of all, I felt heavy remembering a phone call with my ex-husband the day before.   I'd gotten so mad I hung up on him. Truth was, I'd been angry at him for the whole four years we'd been divorced, and probably some before that. I noticed that I was actually slumped over the wheel. Then, out of the corner of my eye, I noticed that the snow was light and pretty. I straightened up and saw more clearly that the night was beautiful. It occurred to me that I didn't need to give my thoughts of Roger all this power... I already divorced him.*

And I laughed out loud.

*I realized all at once that we had enough money; I had a good job, my kids were doing well, why not enjoy life? I also realized in that moment that Roger wasn't quite the ogre I was making him out to be, and that I was sometimes pretty unreasonable. It was not a thought or a feeling, but a sudden realization. **And in that moment everything shifted**. I remember the very store where I stopped and bought pizza. I arrived home happy and my kids asked, "What made you so happy?"*

That simple question the children asked needs to be answered by all of us. In both stories, what made us happy?

... and what makes you happy?

Both of our stories show how our bodies were totally lacking energy. Who we were in our funk was not showing up only in moods, attitudes and responses. Our bodies, minds and spirits were in collapse mode. We were not fun or lighthearted; we were focused on what wasn't working.

We were settling for something less than our best selves. Without knowing it, these were our customary responses to many situations. Interestingly enough, it wasn't how we wanted to live our lives. We are sure you don't either, but it is easy to fall into the trap of looking at the downhearted side of things.

Nancy's daughter saw all the unhappiness in her mom and invited her to play. That joyful teasing transformed Nancy's state. Her snarly self melted away under the thoughts of what was special, more important, and more meaningful to her heart and soul. Nancy yielded to a choice to see the world through her daughter's eyes. Internally, she dropped the straps of indignation that bound her spirit.

Sharon had actually been stuck for a long time, blaming her ex-husband, choosing to remember and respond only to his habits and traits that bugged her. They had the same conversations over and over. It got them both down. Yet they kept reliving the scene.

Sharon felt unlike her real self; she was all slumped over and heavy. Something had to give. The first thing she noticed was that the snow was pretty. It was a first look outside herself. Seeing the beauty of the snow invited Sharon to consider what was real.

Her laughing out loud signaled more than an insight. It was like the internal energy shift of an earthquake. She had devoted so much of her energy to being mad at Roger that she'd lost track of some truths. Their lives were going well. She was free to be happy. So she laughed at her foolish self. And in that moment she was surprised to realize that Roger wasn't as bad as she was holding him to be. Furthermore, she knew she could be pretty impossible herself.

Nancy and Sharon had both shifted. They saw what was previously outside of their vision. With the help of Anita and the snow, they each moved to a fresh perspective. They touched into their innate magic and found freedom and happiness.

So, what is the magic? We may wonder if it is noticing. Or is it discovering what is true? Is it taking off blinders? Is it making a different choice? Is it looking inside? Is it dropping something? Is it picking up something more valuable?

This is a good question for us to consider: **What is the magic that each of us possesses?**

We will help you locate, unearth, then nurture your magic and happiness into fullness. Wouldn't you like to know what's missing?

Let's start with what works.

To begin, we invite you to pause here for a moment and see what is already working well in your relationships. It is meaningful to reflect on what works, because it makes us more hopeful. It also gives us clues to improve other relationships.

We all have relationships, past and present, that are positive. For a moment, think about a particular person who cares about you and values what is important to you. Perhaps you even feel treasured by this person. The person that comes to mind might not be living any longer. That's okay. Is it a family member or a friend? Think about how you cherish them, their wonderful qualities and how they walk through the world. Notice how caring for them adds significantly to your life.

Remember a special moment with this person. Where were you? What was taking place? Enjoy that memory.

What is your experience as you think about them?

Truly let yourself delight in having this person in your life. They live always as a memory in your heart. This memory is yours. Return to it often to feel nurtured.

For us, it is wonderful to recall a dear friend. It is the next best thing to being with them. We breathe easier. Happy feelings well up inside. Remembering our connection, smiles bubble up. We become more alive inside. In this relationship, we feel mutually seen and known, received and grateful. There is space for both to be, to rely on each other, to forgive the inconsequential, to celebrate and grow. Our faith in the relationship carries us through inevitable tensions. We are happy together. Our happiness is the fruit we enjoy from the choices we have made: choices of respect, tolerance, trust, generosity, and good will. Expanding happiness into our other relationships depends upon us making similar choices.

In his book, *The Art of Happiness,* His Holiness the Dalai Lama says: *So, let us reflect on what is truly of value in life, what gives meaning to our lives, and set priorities on the basis of that. The purpose of our life needs to be positive. We weren't born with the purpose of causing trouble, harming others. For our life to be of value, I think we must develop basic good human qualities -- warmth, kindness, compassion. Then our life becomes meaningful and more peaceful -- happier.*

You know how to be in relationship. Trust that. Translating what you know to other relationships will come naturally for you, even if now it seems improbable.

Here's a story from Anna, who found her way to what feels extraordinary:

> *My stepfather, Henry, is a talented architect but he is not a man of words. I had been resisting him pretty much since my childhood. We lived together from my age of 6 to 18, him and me and my mom, and he never asked anything about me. At least that was my perception and how I remembered him. He never knew which grade I was attending, and I thought I was only luggage for him that came along with marrying my mother. He became drunk quite regularly. I was frightened to be close to him.*
>
> *Later, when I seriously fell in love for the first time, he made rude remarks about my boyfriend and me, which I felt were so unjust that I married my boyfriend right after high school and moved out. I just built a wall in myself from which I was keeping him at a distance. I wrote him off.*
>
> *During inner work with Sharon and Nancy, I did a new "search" for nice moments that I remember about Henry. Images came about: their wedding when I felt so happy to be in a family again; making Christmas decorations together with my new sister, him sitting at his huge architect table drawing parts of cities or funny creatures that fascinated me; listening to his playing the piano at celebrations. The most magical memory that came up was my 16th birthday*

when he made a glass organ for me and played "Happy Birthday" and other pieces.

I loved the way he loved great music and became alive and uplifted when listening to or playing Bach.

I also asked this big question: What if he had just 24 hours to live? That really melted my heart towards him. I had a sense that I would like to see him and express my appreciation for him. I offered to show him how the building of a new community complex was going. He designed it and hadn't seen it since the summer, and the scaffolds had just been taken down from around the oval shaped theatre building. It was great to show him "his" buildings. I felt he was proud and I felt proud of him.

Since then we met for a family lunch and I was astonished by the difference of how he was towards me, how my regained respect for him was felt and appreciated by him. He talked to me for almost an hour, although usually he would be silent in the midst of family noise. Actually, I have never ever heard him talk so much, enthusiastically and openly, and specifically to me. When we said good-bye, he rubbed my shoulder gently -- again, the first time in my life, as I remember. I felt genuine and warm affection from him and I feel the same for him.

Anna's early experiences with Henry remind us how easy it can be to travel down a familiar route, even when it's painful. Like Anna, we hold tightly to convincing stories of how we are right. We collect more evidence. We turn away from others rather than step closer to them. Thankfully, Anna's story also suggests how much we can see and remember about what we want most. Anna opened to her stepfather's humanity when she took the blinders off and expanded her heart. Now there was wide-open space created for discovery and connection.

One thing changed, Anna's heart, and the whole relationship changed.

Relationships are at the core of life: families of origin, extended families, families we create, friends, acquaintances, neighbors, co-workers, bosses. We want them to go well. Many of our relationships are positive and fulfilling. Others feel tense, and we don't always know why.

We'll find the answers in our own heart. Our heart gives us access to amazing possibilities for every relationship. We can be happy. We can be at peace.

HEART

Retreat Daily Into Stillness

HEART

NANCY: *Sitting at lunch the other day, my companion was looking beyond me, watching something intently. She turned back to me and described how this little guy around three years old, most probably a grandchild, reached up to hold his grandma's hand. The tenderness between the two of them in that moment was so touching that it brought tears to my friend's eyes.*

Love spreads like a wildfire. It brought a glow to our lunch conversation.

Much of this book is focused on the heart -- getting in touch with it, listening to it and, taking care of it. These days, through all kind of media, we are encouraged to take care of our physical hearts. Magazine articles, TV ads, even billboards urge us to eat right and exercise for our heart's benefit. The heart is a magnificent energy system. Sometimes, however, the energy seems to get stuck. We all have experienced "heavy hearts" as we recounted in our earlier stories. And we also know the joyous feeling of a light heart.

Qigong Master Mingtong Gu says it this way, *When the energy of your heart is expanding, you have a natural feeling of joy, happiness and peace.*

Our hearts are responsive. They are stirred sometimes unexpectedly: like seeing the grandson and grandma at the restaurant, being tickled by gales of laughter bursting from a child, experiencing a joyous flash mob event, meeting by chance a cherished friend from our past, being awestruck by the magnificence of a blazing sunset, or feeling the tender sensations of gratitude.

The joyous expansion of the heart can be contagious, as in Rita's story:

> *We had friends visiting from out of state and we took the local train to the High Museum of Art one Sunday. On the way back home to our station, our train had a problem and we had to get off and get on the train behind ours. The train was packed with lots of people standing. A young family with a small child probably about two years old was in a stroller, and was getting fussy. The train was way too full of strangers for anyone to cope with a crying toddler! One woman, obviously a stranger to the child, leaned over to him and started singing the Sesame Street song. The child was fascinated. Everyone in the train stopped what they were doing to listen. When she got to the end and sang, "Can you tell me how to get, how to get to Sesame Street?" EVERYONE on the train sang! As we finished the last note, the doors of the train opened at the station and we all got off. You could see everyone smiling and I just knew everyone had that same sense of wonder in their hearts that I had. My friend turned to me and said, "I didn't know it was like this in Atlanta." I said, "Today it is."*

We glimpse the heart's joy and feel its persuasive nudges. It invites us to celebrate. Consenting to its call offers us the exalted freedom of sitting on top of the world. By merging joyously in the moment, we connect to everyone, everything, everywhere. Or sometimes our experience might be still, quiet and tranquil, like looking out over a beautiful lake -- feeling that all's right with the world.

The capacity of our own heart is astounding. It is a powerful influential force; it is the seat of emotion, and the inspiration for the poetry of love. The rhythm of the heart is the most basic beat, the foundation of music. It compels us to move, to dance and sing.

Great philosophers and sages extol the heart as the abode of light and love. In the spiritual traditions of many lands, it is said that the heart is the most powerful force. These traditions believe that the great qualities of love, compassion, and joy naturally exist in the heart and connect everything in the universe.

In science, so many discoveries have been made about this complex heart of ours:

- ☐ The heart has a nervous system of its own, sophisticated enough to qualify as a "little brain" in its own right. It can learn, remember, feel and sense.

- ☐ The heart not only receives information from the brain, it sends information to the brain, along 40,000 sensory neurons.

- ☐ Its electrical field is about 60 times greater in amplitude than the electrical activity generated by the brain.

- ☐ The magnetic field produced by the heart is more than 5,000 times greater in strength than the field generated by the brain.

- ☐ The magnetic field of the heart can be detected a number of feet away from the body, indicating that the condition of our heart can actually be "felt" by others.

Author Pete Nelson, in his book, *I Thought You Were Dead*, writes, *Individual heart cells beat at their own rate when separated from one another, a phenomenon easily observed beneath a microscope. It has long been known that when they are pushed together, they will synchronize their pulses. Recent studies have shown, however, that heart cells begin to synchronize slightly before they touch. It is not known how they signal across this distance. Some scientists speculate that this method of communication may be able to cross great distances and may explain how social animals bond, or how pets seem to sense when their masters are coming home, or even how people fall in love, one heart calling to another.*

The study of physics tells us that to change physical matter you have to change either the electrical field or the magnetic field. Science recognizes that the heart does both, even more effectively than the brain. We have underestimated the enormous energy of our hearts.

Having a heart is like owning a golden vessel that holds the most extraordinary power, grander than all the galaxies and all the sciences combined. In caring for this great treasure of ours, in addition to its physical health, many of us pursue uplifting interests or hobbies. For some of us it is movement, activity; for others it is music and art, or spiritual practices. These pursuits return us to balance and give us an expanded view of life. They strengthen the magnetic field of our heart. They nurture our spirit, fueling and shifting our energy. They inspire the great qualities in our hearts to burn brightly, thus helping us see people and our world more graciously. Our perspective opens and embraces beauty, wonder and possibilities.

- ❖ What music makes you sing?
- ❖ What is the rhythm that finds your foot tapping?
- ❖ What movement and activities set you free? Dancing, athletics, sports, yoga, hiking, hobbies, reading, photography, travel?
- ❖ Who are your favorite artists? What do they stir in you? What colors would you love to paint the world?
- ❖ What prayers, blessings, scriptures, books, songs or meditations speak to you?
- ❖ What in nature calls to you the loudest? Mountains, wide-open valleys, caves, oceans, rivers, canyons, forests, animals, flowers, trees?
- ❖ If nature is dear to you, how do you love to commune with it?
- ❖ Pets and inspiring stories are great stimuli as well. Which inspiring stories do you hold in your heart?

Many have heard the story circulated on the Internet about one particular race at a Special Olympics event.

It is told that as the children were running, one child tripped and fell. All the other children racing ahead heard whimpering, stopped their forward course, and went back. They picked up the fallen child. Then they took each others' hands and ran together towards the finish line.

The children innocently and easily saw with their hearts what to do: help the fallen child. They were elated winning together rather than having just one winner.

Can you sense in your heart the selfless compassion and joy that the children experienced?

Without hesitation, these runners' hearts responded to something much grander than a medal for being first. No one lost; the whole group won and felt overjoyed from listening and responding to the whispers in their hearts.

Now you may be thinking all of this sounds like sweetness and light, that we're talking only about children, family, and intimate relationships. Maybe your relationship challenges are at work, and this approach sounds too soft, and not for you. How could something like the heart possibly be effective in a professional and competitive world?

Don't be fooled! The powerful energy of our hearts is like a laser beam that cuts through everything false to reveal the truth about what has been the cause of the problems. It's a different fix from what you have been looking for, and that is why you haven't found it.

All the difficulties in the family, at work, and in the world can be solved with the same selfless compassion the children demonstrated. To the degree we are not in touch with our own heart, we are separate from others and their concerns. Understanding this is essential. There is great advantage in being alive to the relationships that comprise our lives. People's hearts are at the center of every relationship, every interaction, every communication, every deal and contract.

No matter what role you play in the work world, the condition of your own heart matters. Bill O'Brien, late president of Hanover Insurance, spoke of this when he said, *The success of a (business) intervention depends on the interior condition of the intervener.*

Otto Scharmer, the influential MIT business professor, describes a powerful process for use in business that has at its center *Sensing: Connect with your heart.*

The good news is this ability to hear our heart is available to all of us. It is easy to access. It isn't something yet to be attained; we can simply claim all that was previously hidden from our awareness. Listening to our hearts, we will find many endearing and joyous experiences. How do we unlock this wonder?

The Special Olympics team gives us a great clue; we must get clear enough to hear the whispers of our hearts. We need to become like little children, hearts bursting with love and joy, responding spontaneously to the world around us.

How does that happen?

We need to engage intimately with our heart to tap into its vast reservoir. Children have never lost this aliveness. In our busyness, we have become unfamiliar with the most precious of relationships, our relationship with our own heart. An incredible way to discover and strengthen this relationship is through inner stillness.

It is a practice to be still, to listen without need to hear, to simply be free from facts and knowledge, from identification with roles and possessions. What if all was put aside for a moment and we could just rest in the pure unadorned space of "I am"... No pretensions for our sake or others, no claim to glory or victimhood, simply giving ourselves access to what is beneath all that is exterior.

Let's breathe the simplicity of the phrase "I am"... into our whole being a few times. Relax, exhaling slowly and effortlessly. Inhaling, softly say "I am." Again, exhale slowly; inhale "I am." We invite you to do this now several times.

It can feel pretty awkward, exposed and uncomfortable. It's a little like getting naked. Or perhaps for a brief moment, that unadorned concept offers a little freedom. Stay here for a short while at least, and again breathe in the simplicity of "I am."

For these next unhurried repetitions of the phrase, let your vision and body soften, like turning down the volume. As you breathe, allow "I am" to collect in your heart as precious love notes.

Can you sense your heart's pulsations? You might even imagine your heart as a golden vessel ready to be filled to overflowing with recognition and wonder. If you like, you can close your eyes as you practice.

Taking time to truly rest here for longer periods, you can settle down inside yourself. Your mind quiets, creating a softer, spacious state of inner wonder. You are not tethered by thoughts or ideas you have had of yourself. It's as if you are entering an expanded, unexplored state that's not as familiar as your daily routine. Enjoy it.

In this exercise, we are truly encountering our hearts; freed from some frantic effort to be something or someone, to simply be as "I am," calm and content. As we continue this journey, we come to experience who we are at our core, a being of wondrous light and expansive love.

This unchanging "I am" part of our self is always present below the routine way we think and normally function. When we connect with it, we recognize it. It feels ageless. It is a recognition we have of ourselves; we are the one who celebrated our 8-year-old birthday, our high school graduation, and the one that is sitting here and reading this now. We've even heard elders remark, "I know I am 80-something, but I don't feel different or old; I feel like myself."

Perhaps this exercise opened a perspective of timelessness, spaciousness, joy, or maybe a sense of a different or more wonderful you than the usual ways you see yourself. Consistent engagement with the heart creates clearer vision, launching an exploration of knowing that which has been unknown.

Reflecting on the exercise:

❖ What would it be like for you to live from a more relaxed, heartfelt space?

❖ How much easier would it be for others to be with you?

❖ What is the relationship with your heart that you want to create and commit to?

❖ What small, specific practice could support that happening?

❖ From this heartfelt space, how might you interact more easily in relationships?

Regularly taking quiet, still moments inside kindles our own inner radiance. Our lives fill with the energy of enthusiasm, greatness, wonder and joy.

Kim shares a story of one very special moment:

> *I love the mountains and water. This summer a friend and I hiked to a lake we had not been to before. As we sat at the lake's edge, the touch of the earth and heat of the sun seemed to envelop me and share with me its strength and warmth. The wind would rise, whipping the water up in such a manner that the sun reflecting upon it filled it with sparkling diamonds. Then the diamonds would fall and dissolve, bringing the surface of the water to stillness. All my senses were alive to my surroundings, and though I felt small in comparison to the scenery that surrounded me, I also felt large, and an essential part of these beautiful creations. I have often reflected on how fully I felt "me" in that moment. That place in my heart invites me back time and time again.*

We have been talking about the heart as the path to happiness.

Surprising as it may sound, no matter how many things we own or how significant we feel, lasting happiness will not result from those circumstances. Nor will it be found by diminishing ourselves. When we embrace our heart, we begin to understand that pure, genuine essence is alive not only in us, but in each and every person.

And when we respond from our loving heart to the hearts in others, we discover genuine happiness.

This journey takes dedication, commitment to a higher road, humility, and a willingness to change over time. Because this approach is counter to cultural norms, it takes courage and vigilance to stay the course.

Why even commence such a journey?

The answer: to respond to a plea from our heart. There is an intense yearning for peace and joy that whispers to us over and over through our life. Each glimmer of connection increases the longing. Then there comes a time when that soft murmur becomes a cry so loud we cannot ignore or turn away from it any longer. Answering it is a homecoming. It removes self-imposed limits we have presumed about our heart's capacity. We are vastly more than "who we believe" we are, not just a bigger puffed up version. We are capable of experiencing heartfelt connections with others, and a deep sense of belonging.

We are beings of light and love, a subtle, yet powerful energy force that is always pulsing from within our heart. Getting to know that pulsation of love is a homecoming.

Imagine Supreme Longing drawing you home,
restoring you to the astonishing beauty,
the goodness,
the integrity of your own heart.

Like salmon that return to their natal rivers to spawn,
daily immerse yourself in an ocean of love, rest inside --
inside in a haven of stillness.

It is a homecoming to dwell within your own heart,
experiencing freedom and bliss,
knowing who you truly are.

This is where we're headed on this journey: to hear, know, honor, and live from our hearts. The greater this bond to our heart, the more happiness and fulfillment we experience. We become more transparent, authentic and real in our daily projects and relationships. We build our capacity to respond to that which is much grander than winning. We notice ourselves interacting with clearer vision, from a courageous, honest stance. We learn to see with softer eyes. We have a better chance of noticing minute or previously unseen things about ourselves: our reactions, our responses, our behaviors, our thoughts, and more. We even get to discover moods and attitudes while they are still forming.

The more we live from the space of the heart, the more awareness expands and attracts vibrancy, brightening the joy and beauty of each moment. Knowing how to respond to others comes naturally. As a matter of fact, it feels as if we have undoubtedly boarded the right train going in the right direction, more easily meeting the moments of our lives.

As we develop the capacity to remain steadfast in our heart's essence, we invite others into their hearts. The very conditions of our life improve and the extraordinary happiness that is ours flourishes.

MAGIC

Return To Oneness

MAGIC

Here is an allegorical tale:

Truth was walking around the neighborhood, naked. She knocked on several doors. No one would let her in. People would open the door and scream at her nakedness, or just slam the door right in her face. Finally, she knocked on the door of Story, who did let her in. Story clothed Truth in Metaphor and sent her back on her way. Truth again knocked on doors and she was welcomed.

There are many different paths for investigating truth: metaphorically, philosophically, scientifically and from a global humanitarian perspective, to mention a few.

"I heard a nice little story the other day," Morrie says. He closes his eyes for a moment and I wait.

"Okay. The story is about a little wave, bobbing along in the ocean, having a grand old time. He's enjoying the wind and the fresh air -- until he notices the other waves in front of him, crashing against the shore."

"My God, this is terrible," the wave says. "Look what's going to happen to me!"

Then along comes another wave. It sees the first wave, looking grim, and it says to him, "Why do you look so sad?"

The first wave says, "You don't understand! We're all going to crash! All of us waves are going to be nothing! Isn't it terrible?"

The second wave says, "No, you don't understand. You're not a wave, you're part of the ocean."

I smile.

Morrie closes his eyes again. "Part of the ocean," he says, "part of the ocean."

What if the magic referred to in Chapter 1 is Morrie's metaphorical ocean?

In the book and movie, *Tuesdays with Morrie*, we meet Morrie, a thoughtful man nearing the end of his life. He shares his understanding of important things of life through stories. In this process, he becomes philosophical.

Discovering the meaning of things is the pursuit and discipline of philosophy. It is a love of wisdom. It questions beliefs and thoughts in order to solve the problems and questions relevant to our lives. Who am I? Why am I here? Philosophy helps us think about the interrelationship of things in ways we may not previously have considered.

Dr. C. Terry Warner is a contemporary philosopher whose knowledge has had great impact on thinking. In his book, *Bonds That Make us Free*, he says, *To the degree that we become receptive and responsive to the truth, life will keep instructing us. It will teach us all sorts of fresh things about matters we thought we already understood.*

There seems to be a recurrent theme in life that points us towards being receptive to the fresh things that Dr. Warner mentions. We see this in the field of science as well. Scientists update understanding by exploring, studying and discovering more and more about the interplay of the forces of the universe. Science has evidence of things that are difficult to explain. For instance, they have discovered particles (neutrinos) that they can't fully fathom, but know are present. They can measure and even glimpse these particles as the most beautiful blue light ever seen. Science's mission is to explain the world we inhabit. Scientists know they are continually walking the path of further discovery.

In an MIT commencement speech in 1998, President Bill Clinton was speaking about the latest discoveries regarding neutrinos. He emphasized, *The larger issue is that these kinds of findings have implications that are not limited to the laboratory. They affect the whole of society -- not only our economy, but our very view of life, our understanding of our relations with others, and our place in time.*

How do these various perspectives shed light on our idea of magic? In our stories (Nancy's grouchiness and Sharon's anger at her ex-husband) the magic that released our collapsed-funk was not the magic of trickery or sleight of hand. By connecting to something incredibly vital in our hearts, we threw our regrets and resentments out the window. We abandoned our crabby selves. We arrived at peace within ourselves, connected to others, at one with the universe. Magic is not something only available to an elite few; it belongs to all people.

When any of us experience this kind of magic, it often feels both familiar and foreign. It surprises us. We've been here before, but can't remember how we got here. There is a comforting homecoming quality to it. It usually feels wondrous and freeing. How did we stray from this place? How could we have been so close and yet missed it? Perhaps we missed it because this not-easily-described element can't be seen or held in hand; it can only be sensed. And even though it has this kind of subtlety, it is as real as the nose on our face.

Our heart's magic is recognized when we are in tune with it, hidden when we are not present to it. Another name for this magic could be a "oneness" that we all are: some deep-rooted experience of being one soul, one heart, one rhythm pulsing in everything.

It is sometimes puzzling to hold two realities; we know that we are us, separate and uniquely individual, while also having experiences of oneness with others. A classic example of this is meeting someone for the first time, but immediately feeling one with them. Or the example of having exactly the same experience or dream that another person has had. In these examples, we feel connected in surprising ways.

How does that happen? In those moments there is something more that enters our field of possibilities. Dr. Warner reminds us that life *will teach us all sorts of fresh things about matters we thought we already understood.*

What feels normal or usual to us seems to slip away, making room for the unexpected. That is why we refer to it as magic. It has a quality a little like humor. It catches us off guard or outside of what is anticipated. At those moments our hearts' energy is more prominent than the facts stored in our mind. The clear distinctions with which we have defined the world shift. There isn't the usual delineation of where we end and another begins. In those moments we are more than the person we have defined ourselves to be.

> NANCY: *Over 30 years ago, a friend and I discussed a shared desire to engage in a ritual of forgiveness to wash away years of regret. Soon after expressing that wish, we both happened to be in Arizona at the same time. Before our meeting at the Grand Canyon, we each gathered thoughts and precious items to give us strength. When we met together at the rim, awed by its vast depth, we knew it could hold all we were ready to release and consign to it. We meditated, admitted the hurts we had done to others, let go of hurts we blamed others for, and cleared away many of life's unfinished transactions, ones we had regretted.*
>
> *At the conclusion of our ritual, we offered gifts to the canyon. Along with our tears, we offered blessed sage, cornmeal and flower petals. Our hearts overflowed with peace, contentment, jubilation. Feeling absolved, we stretched our arms wide, hands opened to the sky in thanksgiving. Birds came and sat on our hands. It seemed as if nature itself was responding in gratitude to our simple ritual performed at that rim. How harmonious the world felt, one harmonic symphony, one consciousness.*

Deep understanding and respect of oneness with the sun, the moon, the earth and all its creatures is experienced by Native American people. They might express that connectedness this way: the circle of creation is one continuous relationship, all my relations sharing the same breath, the same heartbeat.

The experience of oneness is a taste of innate love. It is not feelings, infatuation or a romantic love. Instead, it is a mysterious, unfettered state that is not only alive in us but resounds in every particle of the universe. It is a pure and infinitely expansive state.

Love is our basic nature. Its memory is always echoing inside us. It creates a longing to be noticed and to experience itself. Like a sound pulse that dolphins send out and receive in the water, we feel or hear love's resonance within us and long to be absorbed in it. The following stories speak to this natural aspiration of our hearts.

NANCY: *A woman was pinned under a city bus in a terrible accident. There were large numbers of responders on the scene and a lot of activity focused on moving the bus and setting her free. One police officer crawled under the bus and saw the woman -- conscious, breathing and really scared. He stayed there with her and held her hand and said that he wouldn't leave until she did. That warmhearted connection was incredibly powerful for the young woman and for the officer. The miracle of their encounter was still palpable when he visited her at the hospital.*

The Make-A-Wish® Arizona Wishletter relates stories of wishes granted to children with life-threatening conditions. Here are accounts of two Arizona boys, who had their wishes granted.

Nine year old Aidan said, "I wish to be a penguin keeper, because I was born loving penguins." In the middle of his wish coming true, Aidan turned to his mom and said, "Mom, I can't stop smiling. My face is starting to hurt."

Liam, age 10, has been in treatment for 3 years. He wanted to meet the "real guys" behind his favorite video game, Call of Duty. He got to sit in a Blackhawk helicopter and learn skills in the simulators. At a ceremony, he received a standing ovation with sixty Army members saluting him. They gave him badges right off their uniforms.

The boys' fulfilled wishes were more than they could have imagined. It was also over-the-top amazing for all the people involved in granting the wishes. Each person's heart was deeply moved. They were offered a taste of oneness.

❖ When was the last time your heart opened wide to someone?

❖ Revisit that experience now. Where were you? What were the circumstances?

❖ Recall it; more than just thinking about it, let yourself re-experience it. What are you feeling now? ... in your heart? ... in your body?

❖ Can you allow yourself to relax even more into the feelings? ... and immerse yourself in them?

It is the process of opening our hearts to others that lets us experience oneness.

Inner love flows from a limitless wellspring. It has more stability than the habits and fortresses of separation that humanity has built up over generations. Our hearts urge us to fulfill the hunger. Our minds keep busy, looking, looking everywhere for *that* satisfaction.

Gratifying that hunger is our primary goal. It is why we are so happy and deeply content when we experience resonance with a piece of music, a profound moment in nature, a healed relationship, a spiritual encounter. Our whole being relaxes; our heart exclaims "yes," affirming how everything feels right, even perfect. Once more, internal, energetic connections are reestablished and strengthened. These moments give us the experience of arriving back home, to what we know and trust as most real.

Imagine One Boundless Pulsation
being the essence of all things,
noticing whatever your eye meets or your mind envisions
simply as one continuous expression
of one conscious energy.

Just as beads of a necklace are strung together;
even more than linked to everything,
your mind-heart-body are in profound communion
with everyone and everything --
you, the space encircling you, the earth, sun, moon and sky
arising from the same spark of consciousness,
reciprocally strung together for one extraordinary experience,
out of one astonishing pulsation.

This most subtle and constant pulse of love continues to awaken and manifest every moment new and fresh. It beats in our heart, pulses through our veins, blinks our eyes, sings through space, throbs beneath the earth, roars on the ocean floor and becomes myriad things and experiences. The more we embrace these magical, yet commonplace, moments and respond with kindhearted love to the people in our lives, the more we will come to know oneness and experience "one" heart.

Love's magic turns the key of our transformation, each pulsation creating a new opportunity.

Each breath is a new beginning, a fresh start, a moment when creation is alive and truth is possible. So powerful and potent, love is able to shake loose habits and tendencies that have bound us. This inborn love delivers us to an expanded state of possibilities.

In everyday life, this magnetic attraction leads us to discover friends and fall in love. We recognize love's whisper. We enter committed relationships because we are deeply aligned, matched like a puzzle piece to another person, and we believe, "That's it, that's what I have been looking for; I have found it." And, then, when our partner doesn't respond the way we want, or points out our imperfections, we push them away saying, "You are wrong. You don't know me. You don't love me." We turn away from the magic, numb to the oneness of love pulsing inside us. We begin another quest to search for the magic that is already standing next to us. How silly we are.

> SHARON: *When I have pulled away from others, I am so self-focused that I literally cannot see anything but myself. I have no ears, no flexibility, no heart, no grace. I was having a conversation with my friend Amy about something in the news. She was insensitive, I felt, missing the big picture. The voice in my head said, "I can't believe she is so blind. She's not as smart or aware as I had thought. I don't want to spend much time with her." Focused on my superiority, I stopped seeing or even being with Amy. Now who was insensitive?*

When we don't have space in ourselves to receive a person, we step away from them in our hearts. We think if we disconnect and dismiss others, we will be safe. Instead our decision limits us. Whether it is co-workers, friends, family or neighbor, our thoughts, actions and attitudes judge rather than understand and embrace. We remain a wave, afraid to merge in the ocean.

> NANCY: *I was already seated at an event as attendees were entering. I was people watching and somehow noticed that my watching wasn't harmless. All around the edges were my thoughts, opinions, comparisons, judgments, and separateness. It was as if in an instant I woke up, catching myself with my hand in the cookie jar. And then this new thought appeared: You have no idea what is in the heart of each person. What a humbling moment. Given new eyes, I began to see hearts entering the room. My heart softened and I experienced "all my relations." It felt sacred.*

What an incredible stance to adopt. "Oneness" matters and is key in the transformation of relationships. It's something we've experienced before. In relating to others, we've all had moments of knowing this powerfully connected feeling, this "oneness." Perhaps it was at the birth of a child, celebrating a dear friend's long-awaited success, or in a more everyday experience such as being touched by a person's unexpected kindness.

These moments of love sometimes arise from shared, sacred experiences, sometimes in response to external situations like attending the wedding of a dear friend. When we nurture our internal expansion of oneness, love springs naturally and unsolicited from deep within our own hearts. We can become so fluent that love is our instinctive response to others. No matter what another person's state may be, our rootedness in being "one" heart with them will outweigh any resistance in us.

This is the true definition of vulnerability with another person. It is a state of fearlessness, a powerful perspective that trusts in ourselves and others. No longer do we need to shield our heart to protect ourselves. As our innate state of love becomes more constant, shifting our hearts in difficult moments becomes easier. A Native American chant can escort us to this space now.

Relax into your breath, inhaling and exhaling softly with ease. When you are ready, gently bring your awareness to your heart. You might like to place your hand or hands lightly over your physical heart to increase this awareness. Do you notice or hear its cadence? Take your time.

Now, allow your heart to fill with the radiant light of this Navajo chant:

Deep inside your heart resides boundless love, splendid power, and vast wisdom. Immerse yourself. Beauty surrounds you and enfolds you in an ocean of serenity. Let all thoughts dissolve into an expansive and luminous silence and enter oneness. Dwell here for a few moments.

This that is beautiful, it shows my way;
This that is beautiful, it shows my way;

Before me is beautiful, it shows my way;
Behind me is beautiful, it shows my way;

This that is beautiful, it shows my way;

Above me is beautiful, it shows my way;
Below me is beautiful, it shows my way;

This that is beautiful, it shows my way;
This that is beautiful, it shows my way.

Absorbed in this place of wonder, notice your experience.

We are on a journey to uncover all we haven't seen yet, in the same way that philosophy and all the sciences keep discovering more about the universe. As we peel back layers of division, we will experience the love that has been there all along. It will become apparent how being deaf to our hearts' whispers impacts our relationships. When we look in the right way, we will find the answers.

Here is a tale from a compilation of humorous oral stories handed down about Mullah Nasrudin. The title, "mullah," is used as a term of respect for a man thought to be very wise. However, this beloved character is known for his antics, by children and adults alike, throughout the Middle East and Central Asia. Much of the time he is the fool making us laugh at his lack of common sense or outrageousness.

Sometimes he reveals deeper truth about our lives.

Someone saw Nasrudin searching for something on the ground.

"What have you lost, Mulla?" he asked. "My key," said the Mulla. So they both went down on their knees looking for it.

After a time the other man asked, "Where exactly did you drop it?"

"In my own house."

"Then why are you looking here?"

"There is more light here than inside my own house."

Isn't it great that over and over in our daily lives, even when we have lost the key, something as profound as love's oneness knocks again at our awareness? A co-worker stops to chat; our child wants us to play; we receive three voice mails from the same person; all are bidding us to return to our heart.

Please bring to your mind a person whom you might be overlooking, a person who longs for you to appreciate them.

- ❖ What lets you know their hunger? Is it something they say? Is their behavior begging for your attention? Could it be a whisper you hear in your heart?
- ❖ What are their great qualities? How have you seen love shine through them?
- ❖ Can you recognize the longing in their heart?
- ❖ In what ways are they more similar to you than different?
- ❖ How have you let them know they are not worthy of your love?

In this moment put aside all the questions and answers. Know that the same love that exists in your heart exists in their heart as well. Reverently hold this thought.

What if each of us could become aware of our own and other people's innate beauty and goodness? What if we could see the similarities in all people, even those who live far away or live by different beliefs? What if we got good at seeing past our differences to our shared humanity? How might our lives and the whole world change?

The Zen Buddhist Monk, Thich Nhat Hanh, explains, *We are here to awaken from the illusion of our separateness.*

It is possible to prepare ourselves, our mind and heart, for such an Olympian task.

MIND

Make It Your Friend

SHARON: *This was a week of many small irritants. My dishwasher gave out, my car had to be towed, my brother-in-law, Garfield, whose finances I handle, was anxious and forgetful and called me about twenty times a day to review what I'd just told him. And to add to all that, the city is replacing the gas lines on our street and the continual noise is jarring.*

Have you ever noticed how sometimes the most aggravating things can just roll off your back? It is as if you are in some kind of heightened state that isn't affected by outer circumstances. We hope there are many times when you experience a state of incredible expansion and oneness with everyone, as if all is right in the world. This state comes with such a liberating feeling, full of clear vision, generosity and compassion.

Then there are the other times when the same event, perhaps not even as aggravating, affects us quite differently. We are bothered, defensive, judgmental, critical, and standoffish. What creates that difference? The answer is: **The state of our mind.**

The mind is most mysterious. It does not have physical form like the brain. Therefore, some people have questions about its existence.

A 2014 article written by a long list of illustrious academics, one of whom is Dr. Deepak Chopra, highlights the quest to understand the mind: *For twenty years a conference bubbling with enthusiasm has taken place in*

Tucson to figure out the origins of the human mind. Its title is: Toward a Science of Consciousness. As you can imagine, it's not an easy problem for science to solve. What moment of the day isn't involved in the mind?

Technological advances, especially in the field of neuroscience, have allowed for huge strides in understanding the physical apparatus of the brain. Scientists are now watching, measuring, and identifying the workings of the brain in real time, which is impressive! Many of these scientists believe that when we fully understand the brain, we will understand the mind. We think not. That is like saying that to understand the impact Beethoven's Ninth Symphony has on us, we must understand the radio (or other device) through which it is playing.

Dr. Chopra and his colleagues remind us, *The entire area of reality that includes the self, mind, truth, beauty, idealism, compassion, and all other human traits – including the negative ones – is nonphysical.*

We uphold the position that the mind does indeed exist. It enables us to have subjective awareness and intentionality towards our environment, to perceive and respond to stimuli with some kind of agency, and to have consciousness, including thinking and feeling. The mind is both a mystery and a treasure. It is extremely important to us. Without our mind, we can't carry out everyday tasks such as driving, preparing a meal, answering e-mails, or placing a call. Without the mind, we cannot function. We cannot even recognize our friend.

Eastern yogic psychology describes the mind and its functions in a way that will add to our understanding. **The mind:**

☐ **Collects and recognizes information** (Intellect -- the function that collects information from the senses; it also differentiates day/night, man/woman.)

> Our five senses bring to our attention information from the environment around us. We hear raindrops on the roof, see spring bursting with color, taste the coolness of water, smell the scent of perfume, and we feel the wind on our face. Information comes without opinion, just clear sensation. We recognize the input because of our mind's

ability to receive impressions through our sense organs. Also, sometimes our senses are receiving information we don't yet recognize. With the input from the thinking faculty, the intellect has the capability to discern, clarify and bridge understanding.

☐ **Matches that information with previous experience** (Thinking faculty -- collects thoughts from memory.)

Each sensory item taps into a data bank based on our own accumulated collection of thoughts and past associations. It sends this information back to the intellect to make some judgments. Is the person walking up to the door a relative or a stranger? Why is the liquid in this glass colored? Is it water or a flavored drink?

☐ **Interprets the information relationally** (Identifier -- connects us to the world.)

It is crucial for us to understand that an important function of the mind is to decide what sensory input means to us. We weigh the information based on our outlook in the moment, our preferences, our past experiences, and meaning that we attribute to the input. Some things, people and experiences we like, and some we don't. If we planned a picnic, we might not like the raindrops we hear. A rainy day might change our mood from light to dark. Or perhaps there has been a long drought and the sound of raindrops becomes a delight; we feel relief and gratitude.

This example shows these three functions working together: First, we smell the scent of flowers, which draws our attention to the flower shop. Secondly, we remember the beauty flowers add to a room and that guests are coming for dinner. Thirdly, we go into the shop and begin to choose the flowers we love the most. This third function is most interesting. This is where the "I am" that we worked with earlier starts to add on to its pure, unsullied state. The identifier makes decisions about how it wants to be in relationship with the information.

It does this by using the information it gathered in the first two functions. Its desire might be to own, or become attached to the object, or feel an aversion to it. "I like this flower, this one is ugly; this is mine, this is not mine; this is my friend, this is not my friend." This third function, the identifier, points us one more time to the fact that we are in constant relationship with the world, choosing how we will think about and relate to it.

So how do we know we have a mind?

We experience the world around us: Creative thoughts and ideas come to mind. We have day dreams and big hopes. We figure out complex situations.   We think of the people we love and care about. We feel uplifted by the thoughts in our mind, or they can be the source of our suffering. Let's look a little more deeply at thoughts that take us down a dark path.

> SHARON: *Sitting at the airport, I didn't know any of the people, yet I noticed I had really quick and often harsh judgments about them. I even imagined the kinds of people they were: "I can't believe that woman wore that dress to the airport." "That family is paying no attention to their child who is rummaging through the garbage. How irresponsible!" "The woman over there looks like someone I would like." "I don't even know that man, but I heard him on his cell phone and I don't like him a bit."*

Sharon's story is familiar. Do you ever notice the way your mind compares, judges and comments? Let's pause to ponder these questions:

- ❖ How do I carry harshness into life?
- ❖ What is the impact of my judgments?
- ❖ How might critical thoughts affect my life?
- ❖ Might others sense my critical mind?
- ❖ How are others not deserving of my demeaning thoughts?

NANCY: *Several years ago, I was struggling to have a friend respond to me in the way I wanted. I could feel myself sliding little by little down the slippery slope of trying to change her. I noticed the speed building, just a bit at a time, so that I hardly could be bothered by what I was doing.*

Then before I knew it, kaboom! I landed at the bottom of an emotional slope, consumed by what I was sure were awful things that she was doing. I felt self-righteous about it. I became really angry. I wanted her to be wrong; I could hardly think of anything else. I blew everything out of proportion and kept building a story with all its exaggerations.

We know we have a mind because it works so hard supporting and sustaining "reality" as we see it.

It incessantly repeats unhappy scenarios. We agonize over all of them. What makes the mind a hindrance is that it is in constant activity. Its voice chatters away, commenting about our ability or inability to do things, noticing this person or that, often making judgments, or at least comparisons. It can produce endless lists. It wants to figure things out and make decisions, sometimes waging war with "either-or" arguments: yes or no, should I?/shouldn't I? The mind can become so harried that sometimes it is a struggle to keep it focused on what we are doing.

What is also important to us in the study of the mind is how it creates our reality. Rabindranath Tagore, the first non-European to win the Nobel Prize in literature, articulates his view on the mind by saying, *Most people believe the mind to be a mirror, more or less accurately reflecting the world outside them, not realizing on the contrary that the mind is itself the principal element of creation.*

NANCY: *I had climbed a mountain and was descending, when I had a terrible fall. Catching the weight of my fall on my hand, I was in excruciating pain all the way up into my neck. My hiking buddy got me to a nearby healing practitioner that she trusted.*

He told me to take off my shoes and leave them at the door. I thought that strange, but I also was not thinking clearly, so I followed his direction without questioning. I got up on his table and he looked me in the eyes and said what he was going to do was going to hurt a lot only if my mind stayed in my body. He told me to take my mind and put it in my shoes. Looking back now, that seemed like the simplest direction, like someone asking me to smile or shake their hand. I did it that simply. I have no idea what manipulations he did; they were pain-free. I walked out of the office feeling really well.

Nancy's story illustrates the immense power of the mind. Given the circumstances, the practitioner helped Nancy access that power. On the other hand, we often don't know our mind's power or what the outcome will be from following our minds' thoughts and desires. We want to live in more sunshine. We move to the desert where the sun always shines and then are upset in the heat of the summer. We like someone and want to partner in a project with them; then we can't stand to be with their idiosyncrasies.

All the fluctuations of our emotions arise from the thoughts in our mind: Happy/sad, fearful/secure, grateful/discontented, anxious/ peaceful.

We are the ones that spin the roulette wheel and decide how to play, based on how we conceive of, interpret and connect to our thoughts. We can be pulled around the block by a mind that is not steady, like an untrained Great Dane dragging us around on his leash. We must be discerning. If we lack sharpness of vision, clarity of purpose, and gentle self-discipline, the mind can make our life a nightmare.

Here is an enjoyable story that demonstrates these ideas:

There was a poor vagabond wandering though the backwoods of India. Tired, hungry and exhausted, he unknowingly sat down under the shade of a wish-fulfilling tree. He fell into a deep sleep and when he awoke, he thought about what it would be like to have a better life.

He wished to be a king, and in an instant he became a king. He wished for a beautiful woman to enjoy this glorious experience with him. To his surprise a most gorgeous women sashayed up to him. The man, now a king possessing gold and riches, remembered that he was in a remote area, near a forest. He thought how horrible it would be if a tiger came and devoured him. Sadly, in an instant, he was in the jaws of a tiger!

Are we a little daft like this man, unaware of the power of our mind and how all our jumbled, cascading thoughts create uncomfortable realities for us? This man could have gone on enjoying the fulfillment of his great wishes. However, his mind was wild and untamed. It drifted aimlessly.

The purpose of the mind is to think, to serve us, not to pull us this way and that. This poor man's mind became his enemy because it was in charge; it strayed wherever it pleased, chasing after desires and inventing fear. The same can happen for us, since our minds are the drivers of our lives.

Our minds can conjure up thoughts, wishes, scenarios, anxieties, even torments. They also can be burdened by unflattering thoughts about ourselves and others which we actually believe to be true. All the undesirable tendencies that drain our energy are the result of self-conditioning. We choose to think in convenient, predictable patterns, filtering out what feels irrelevant to our perspective. We form habits from making the same choices over and over again. What an incredible waste of the wealth of this phenomenal mind.

The mind is there to serve us in myriad ways. It can take us to the highest joy. It can unfold answers to the mysteries of life. It can help progress the evolution of mankind. It can imagine and create beauty. The mind can solve intractable problems. It can generate love and peace. It can free us and others from suffering. It can inspire our greatness. It can expand into bliss... And this list continues. The mind has the power to be steady, strong, fearless, discerning, able to focus, and to create harmony.

What if we made our mind our friend?

How exceptional life would be if we reaped the mind's benefits. A wholesome mind is like a finely tuned instrument that resonates clearly. Our mind needs to be toned and have great resonance for us to have a wonderful life experience. One of the powerful ways to strengthen it is to get better and better at noticing our thoughts, and becoming aware of their effects. It takes courage and discipline to notice. Not the beat-yourself-up variety of discipline, instead, a commitment to helpfulness.

Our continual care and attention supports the mind's capacity to become tranquil, clear and responsible, a creative, magnetic current of life. As we relinquish our worries and fears, the mind becomes more serene and able to support our desire for happiness.

Imagine Crystal Clarity radiant as the sun,
soothing your heart,
whispering to you,
inspiring serenity and kindness.

Just as bird-songs brighten spring skies,
free your mind from disheartening patterns and thoughts.

Choose light, uplifting thoughts --
ones that sparkle, enliven, gladden your spirit,
filling you with peace and joy.

Daily doses of quietude give the mind vital nourishment. Just as our bodies can't endure working out all day, mental and emotional overload are detrimental. When the mind is continually wound tightly in thoughts and concerns, it loses elasticity, perspective, and capacity to see and make decisions effectively. Our minds need rest; solace from constant activity. Inner silence replenishes the cells and lures the mind back to its true essence as naturally as bees are drawn to wildflowers. A composed mind is always just one breath away. It is a decision we make. As we develop our relationship with inner serenity, our mind will function optimally.

Laughter and play, as well, are essential for a healthy mind. They release tension and seriousness, while creating a light heart and happiness. People participate in a wide variety of playtime activities -- creative endeavors, games, and sports, to name a few.

> NANCY: *During a recent group InterPlay exercise, we began by individually getting to "know" just one of our hands -- shaping and reshaping it, tightening and releasing, moving it to lighthearted music. Playing in this simple way dissolved all else. In this quiet activity, my body relaxed, thoughts melted away, and openness and joy bubbled up. I felt satiated, full, revitalized not needing anything else. Neither questions nor answers mattered, just experiencing "being" was enough. Then we joined the group with this newfound friend (our own hand) to hand-dance with each other. Our play sparked more happiness and deep connection.*

Relaxing into the mind's pure nature unveils the magic of oneness.

His Holiness the Dalai Lama speaks about the mind's clarity as "clear light" and that its essential nature is pure. In this pure, expanded state the mind witnesses. It sees the world through our eyes, being unaffected by what appears. It watches moments unfold, like a curious child filled with wonder.

Witnessing is a transparent view of the world from inside out, drawing no conclusions and pronouncing no verdict on what it sees. It simply notices. It unearths the mysteries lying beneath the surface. It is the one processing the words on this page, the one who identifies scents, who recognizes feelings. It is as if a fog clears away, colors awaken and nature glistens.

Our journey together is to return the mind to its essential nature.

CONSCIOUS

Choose Carefully

CONSCIOUS

NANCY: *Anita is visually impaired. When she was a toddler, her dad was carrying her on his shoulders one early spring day. As they brushed under one of the giant oak trees in the yard, she exclaimed, punctuating each word, "Oh! Trees. Have. Leaves." Although that happened many, many years ago, that moment has stayed with me because of how it awakened me. In that comment, I heard an almost sightless child merge what she noticed with several facts and understandings into a new reality. Over the years I have contemplated its innocent and layered implications.*

We take our sight and all our senses for granted. We distinguish between things: it is day and not night; it is cold enough to wear a jacket; a pair of shoes does not fit; we have a headache; what we communicated had a different impact from what we intended. We make associations and connections between things. We are inundated with "unpacked" experiences interacting with each other. In this way, we continually process our understanding of life, whether it is well-founded or not.

SHARON: *Here is a March journal entry: I'm startled when something wakes me up and I suddenly notice lots of things. I have just finished my 19-day Baha'i Fast. For 19 days every March, we don't eat or drink anything between sunrise and sunset. I used to think it was a dreadful inconvenience at the least. Other times I thought it was torture. Somehow over the years its meaning has changed and, although it takes some mental and spiritual preparation, now it's not hard and I actually like it. It jolts my routines and I see a lot of things I've been blind to.*

I watch the sunrise with new eyes, and enjoy noting that the time of sunrise doesn't change evenly. Some days it's one minute earlier, some days two. The morning bird symphony is striking! On my walk today all the blossoms on Chestnut Street were in full bloom. Yesterday the branches were just sticks. When I take the first sip of water at sunset, it is glorious and I think it is the first time I've ever really tasted water. I nearly swooned over a nut yesterday.

This heightened awareness, this keen noticing that seems to come with fasting makes me wonder how many other things in my life I'm blind to. I wrote an e-mail to a client. He wrote back all confused. As I was patiently responding, it occurred to me to reread my initial e-mail. I was shocked. My e-mail made no sense at all. How often am I blind to myself? Blaming the other person for what may well be my flaws?

Self-discovery is a great place to continue expanding awareness, since this journey called life is taking place within our hearts, bodies and minds. When we open to discovery, we find so many established routines, likes and dislikes, tendencies, preferences, dependencies, strengths, weaknesses, and capacities. All of these influence how we notice each moment throughout the day.

Leo Strauss, a philosopher, gives us a window into a whole new vista we might want to consider: *All there is to thinking is seeing something noticeable, which makes you see something you weren't noticing, which makes you see something that isn't even visible.*

Pondering this quotation, it is good to consider: How conscious am I, throughout the day, of the world I inhabit? To what am I not awake? Did I notice a stranger's smile? Did I see the stars in the sky last night? What color are my friend's eyes? What else might I be missing along the journey?

Leo Strauss follows the whole path from being blind and not knowing it, to seeing, and then beyond to experiencing what can't be seen. Maybe the biggest invisible thing that people can feel is the condition of each other's heart. If someone is acting all sweet, but underneath they're angry, we know. What is more important for us to notice, though, is when *we're the one* who's offering anger or a mixed message. If we want our relationships to work well, it is crucial for us to notice our thoughts, our actions, and the condition of our hearts.

Awareness is the first step. It is a subtle, silent study.

Awareness requires presence, respect, deceleration, openness, discernment, and patience. Presence. Respect. Deceleration. Openness. Discernment. Patience. When we slow down and elevate our way of seeing to a purer level, more aligned with the energy of consciousness itself, we embrace that "clear light" to which the Dalai Lama refers. It makes no judgments. This awareness reveals a world usually unseen by our physical eyes.

Imagine including a subtle and more delicate vision, by becoming the one who watches. Rather than looking for anything or analyzing, practice being fully present: observe with sensitive, expanded awareness. What are the clues our bodies are giving us? Is our stomach churning, our jaw tight, our words audible, deafening or sarcastic, our torso contracted? Are we relaxed, friendly, able to listen?

Becoming conscious, aware, is fundamental to making wholesome progress in life. This includes being aware of others' hearts and needs, of our environment, of our thoughts, our behaviors and our impact in relationships. Martin Buber, a 20th century philosopher, believed that the only way to become truly whole is through being aware and present in the unfolding of our relationships with others.

Ivan struggled in his relationship with his partner. His story speaks about becoming more aware:

> *I consider the dilemma my partner is in regarding the decisions she must make in pursuing her career as a midwife: being away for long hours, having to go to a different city to get trained, and possibly having to move to a different part of the country when she qualifies. This means a whole series of*

> *changes are possible for her, her son, and me. My being more vibrant, loving, clear and supportive would ease that load.*

There is power available in seeing our relationships and the world as they are, not as we want them to look. It takes a certain kind of care and attention. An expanded perception provides much information. It gives us the ability to unknot habitual patterns and create more freedom in our lives. It influences how we respond to the people and world around us.

Expanded perception is the gateway to transformation.

To adopt this kind of vision, great advice has been given to us by Mary Burmeister, a master of the art of Jin Shin Jyutsu. *Look until you can HEAR. Listen until you can SEE.* This type of awareness has us step utterly quietly into what Leo says "... isn't even visible." When our awareness becomes this subtle, our heart is fully engaged, steady and available. The mind and the heart are working together intimately; they shine as one clear source of light. The experience of love's oneness is felt when our hearts connect with other people. What better happiness can we experience?

With this kind of gentle, kindhearted noticing, change is already afoot. Shifts begin to happen. Something that was more solid in us softens and opens space. AND this space creates the possibility of making choices. We become conscious of choices, from simple ones to those increasing in significance: water or soda? chocolate or lunch? sandwich or salad? rest our eyes or press on? listen or be busy? worry or trust? feel righteous or apologize? follow a dream or pick a secure career? respond to another's heart or turn away?

Every minute of every day we have the ability to make choices about *what* to do and *how* to do it, *what* to think and *how* to think, and literally, *how* to be with others. It is extraordinary to truly grasp that we have so much power.

We get to choose.

As a matter of fact, whether or not we are consciously choosing, choosing is happening. We usually do not recognize or experience all the choice points. With really big things it might be easier to notice: *What shall I do with the rest of my life? Shall I marry this person?* It's harder to realize we are choosing in every moment on little, everyday things like choosing chocolate or lunch. However all choices are significant. The choices we make affect us and our relationships.

> SHARON: *I like doing things my way, wanting others to SEE my way. Yesterday a client of mine was upset because he'd just had a big fight with his wife. He said, "All I want is for her to acknowledge me." I asked him, "Did the fight help her acknowledge you?"' He looked defeated and said, "No, if anything, it proved that she shouldn't." This exchange had me reflect: How might it feel for the other person, when I cut a conversation short, like I did with Rudy today, because I couldn't get him to see things my way? It is clear that my choice was turning away from Rudy and what mattered to him.*

Let's go back to **the chocolate or lunch choice** for another moment: **What goes into making that choice?** Is there thoughtfulness? Is there convenience? Is there desire? Is there awareness of how choosing either chocolate or lunch will affect us? ... and others? What are the underlying intentions of our life that influence this choice? If we don't have a clear intention, how will we know how to choose?

The choice seemed so simple in the moment. We felt a pang of hunger, boredom or frustration. However, our deeper look asks this question, "Who am I?" If we haven't clearly understood and embraced that we are an amazing being having a golden opportunity on earth, we might be acting unconsciously. Then the choice we make in the moment has more to do with the untrained Great Dane dragging us wherever he wants to go.

All this chocolate and lunch conversation isn't intended to make you hungry, or to make a judgment about one choice being better than another, but to emphasize how important choice and intention are. Our choice actually might be to choose both. However, are we aware as we choose?

The most basic and deep-seated understanding we have to reach is to truly know who we believe ourselves to be, and how we want to live this precious life. We know what our heart is yearning for; we have heard its whispers. Once we claim that with certainty, clear choice and change are possible in all areas of our lives.

> NANCY: *I met a young man from New York at a conference several years ago. There was something about his energy that was compelling and impressive. He told me his amazing story: He had been working on setting goals for his life, more honest and loving ways he wanted to live with the people he cared for. One decision he made was to remove the automatic "no" from his responses. On the morning of 9/11, his young daughter asked him if they could go out to breakfast together. The automatic "no" came up inside as he thought about all the work on his desk in the tower. Remembering his recent commitment to his loved ones, he decided he could be late for work. He turned to her and said, "Yes, let's do that."*

This one choice radically changed his world. Moved by this story, if you haven't answered the "Who am I?" question yet, please settle now on one reason you are here on earth. Encapsulating this in a word or two is important. The still place in your heart knows the "why." It knows what it is your heart wants to express. It might be the one thing you hope others will remember about you after you are gone. Or it might be the quality you admire most in other people. It can be something as basic as generosity, wisdom or kindness. It will show up as a recurrent theme in your life. All other intentions in your life will rest comfortably upon this. Life will feel harmonious.

Once that first step is done, we are ready to create the best for our relationships. Let's become crystal clear about how we want to be with the people in our lives. Discerning choices change our lives. Take time to sincerely contemplate each question:

- ❖ How do I want my relationships to improve? How do I want to be? How will success look and feel?
- ❖ What will this outlook provide for me?

❖ How will others benefit?

❖ Who are the specific people who will be affected? How will my improvement help them?

❖ What is the internal shift I need to make in order to hold and honor all my relationships?

❖ What is an intention that compels me to be all I can be in relationships?

❖ How can this intention be such an irresistible vision, so meaningful to me, that my whole being consents to it?

❖ How can I dedicate myself to this intention?

REMEMBER: To help improve your relationships, this intention will be your guide. In order to honor it, please become succinct and record it.

We are on our way to freeing what has been stuck. We have focused on awareness and intention because that pair sets the stage. Let's look at the choices that impact relationships in sustainable ways. They are subtle.

We'll begin with an analogy to help us grasp these subtle choices.

Think about the magic of the giant sunflowers. They are totally amazing and beautiful, full of sensitivity and flexibility. They live their lives relating to the sun. In the morning they open their wide-eyed faces to the east and as the day progresses, they continue to turn, following the sun's luminosity. From sunrise to sunset they are easefully and respectfully focused on their relationship with the sun.

Taking a lesson from these tall friends can help us to make progress in our relationships. We can't just muscle ourselves into some new plan to forward our intention, much as we may try. The choice that ensures sound relationships is more than simply a one fell swoop change in behavior. Changing a relationship in a lasting way involves a chain of considerations, (like stepping stones across the river,) a succession of choices that creates a whole.

Here is the step which is vitally important. We must relax into our heart, soften into our intention and become flexible. It is a surrendering similar to the devoted connection of the flowers to the sun. What helps most is letting go of thoughts and opinions that have held our heart at bay, giving us reason to resist the turning of our heart. We must soften into a different "interior condition." Taking time to reflect on this new dynamic of our intention, we begin to hear truth whispering to us, calling us back to oneness.

Like the sunflowers, we need to be on the journey, guided by the beam of light from the other person's heart. We reaffirm our desire to grow, to expand more into connection and our own light. We grow aware of how inflexible we have become, and soften more. We begin to see the other person's heart with new, sensitive eyes. We allow ourselves to hear our own subtle, inner guidance.

Then, quite naturally, we know who we can be and need to be in this relationship. What we can do for the person becomes clear. This responsive impulse to act arises from an internal metamorphosis, having followed many stepping stones of fresh perceptions and choices. The river of incremental choices has been successfully crossed, connecting us more deeply to our heart and our intention.

The choice is to act.

When our hearts are engaged with people, and our clear intention fuels our thoughts and our actions, we are operating from the strongest heart-mind connection imaginable. This stance has immense power for making everything possible.

Only one thing changes: our heart, and the whole world changes.

Lynne Twist, a global visionary, gives us a great model. She and her family made a wholehearted commitment to end world hunger. As a result, everything Lynne chooses is colored by this intention. As an author, global lecturer, and fund raiser, she has both highlighted hunger in the world and spearheaded solutions. Lynne's attention is on her intention. Her example hands this beacon of light onward to us.

Are you ready to live everyday life in an extraordinary way?

Can you hold firmly to your intention, your inspiring vision of being in relationship?

Enjoy this beautiful anecdote from the life of Mother Teresa, from Christina Stevens book *Love:*

> *During the period when West Beirut was under siege, Mother Teresa felt strongly about getting in to see to the needs of the people. Priests and officials explained to her that it was a good idea, but impossible.*
>
> *Holding firm to the deep desire still churning in her heart, Mother Teresa visited the American Ambassador. He told her there would need to be a cease-fire. She said she had been praying for that to happen and that she was certain the cease-fire would occur. He was so charmed by what he saw as her innocence that he immediately agreed to help her when the cease-fire happened. Of course it did, and now faced with this predicament he wasn't at all sure what a nun could do in such an intense and war-torn situation.*
>
> *Their convoy arrived at a hospital that housed sixty physically impaired children who were frightened, and alone, without any adults or the care they needed. Mother Teresa just started embracing and carrying each child, one by one, out to the Red Cross vans.*
>
> *A day after the rescue, the children's faces were full of smiles because someone cared. Mother Teresa said, "Not all of us can do great things. But we can do small things with great love. ... It is not what we do; it is how much love we put in the doing. It is not what we give; it is how much love we put in the giving."*

Mother Teresa was an amazing, heart-centered woman, who responded over and over to whispers she heard in her heart. She looked until she could hear, and listened until she could see. Because of that conviction, she believed possible what other people saw as impossible. In her early days as a nun, many people felt that there was nothing extraordinary about her. Mother Teresa was an ordinary person who responded in humble, yet extraordinary ways. Her intention was so clear that nothing stopped her.

How might Mother Teresa inspire your heart's commitment to your intention?

- ❖ How could you have a generous heart toward others more often?

- ❖ What simple act of kindness is your heart asking you to offer to someone you love?

- ❖ What simple act of kindness is your heart asking you to offer to someone who is difficult for you to love?

- ❖ What would you have to believe so completely about your capacity to love that nothing could divert your attention?

- ❖ How might you expand your love?

Another visionary, Nelson Mandela, president of South Africa, was so determined to make a difference for the people of South Africa that it shifted his combative posture to being the ultimate listener. He became committed to understanding the other side's concerns in order to make decisions and do the right thing. This impressive shift took place because Mandela allowed his intention for equality to transform him.

Are you willing to allow your intention for peaceful, loving relationships to transform you?

The best of history has happened because Gandhi, Martin Luther King, Rosa Parks, Mother Teresa, Lynne Twist, Nelson Mandela and many others, people just like us, held fast to their visions, believing with all their being that what they dreamed and intended was possible. Their hearts were fully engaged. They weren't concerned with what they might have to do or how they would personally benefit. Instead, their greatness occurred because they offered themselves respectfully and unsparingly. They were using the creative power of their minds in the best of ways. Their spirited visions became lived experiences through moment to moment choices they made.

Imagine Mystifying Time always on its own schedule,
quite untameable,
wearing its own watch, singing its own tune.

Rather than cursing a blustery wind
carrying away your hat,
hold every moment as auspicious,
respecting each minute's blessings,
consciously stepping into unknown worlds.

Dancing to your heart's content,
take responsibility for the music you hum,
intentionally creating --
grateful for each blossom.

When we live from the deepest intention in our heart, accentuated by our feelings and enthusiasm about that purpose, then nothing can stop us.

Hold onto and already taste the reality of peace, love and compassion in your relationships. Believe that your vision is important. Its energy will unfold what is necessary to accomplish it. See it already as the life you are living. Be prepared to have a change of heart.

RESOLVE

Expand Your Capacity To Love

RESOLVE

SHARON: *At a conference I attended years ago I saw a short video. There were six people -- three in white shirts and three in black shirts -- tossing basketballs around. We were instructed to watch carefully and silently count the number of passes made by the white shirted players. I did as instructed, and was proud to have counted 17 passes. Then the presenter asked, "How many of you saw a gorilla in the video?" There was tittering. I would have bet $500 on the spot there was no gorilla. The video was replayed. To my utter astonishment, a person dressed as a gorilla strolled right through the middle of the action, faced the camera, thumped its chest, and then strolled off. I was so amazed that I purchased the video from Viscog and showed it at many workshops. Typically less than a quarter of the audience saw the gorilla.*

How can we miss a gorilla? Something could be said for the ability to be focused, but it is startling to realize what we might be missing. Following the instructions, Sharon's mind, not her eyes, ignored the gorilla. In many ways, we have conditioned our minds. In so doing, we have locked ourselves into creating the same, familiar realities, rather than embracing the mind's greater capacity.

Our awesome, wondrous hearts will help our minds comprehend what we haven't previously understood.

The familiar tale of the elephant and blind men illustrates this well. As told on the Peace Corps website, there were six blind men arguing about what an elephant is.

These six men quarreled, each believing their opinion was correct: "An elephant is a giant," one proclaimed. Another argued, "No, it's a gentle being since a princess can sit atop." Another was certain an elephant was something magical. Finally the villagers felt this disagreement needed to stop, so they escorted the six blind men to a nearby palace to visit the king's elephants. Each man touched the elephant and became more certain of his view. The arguments not only continued, but grew louder. So loud, in fact, that they woke the Rajah from his afternoon nap. "The elephant is a very large animal," said the Rajah kindly. "Each man touched only one part. Perhaps if you put the parts together, you will see the truth."

The parts that we will be putting together in this and the remaining chapters of the book are the powerful energies of our minds and hearts. Married together, they can help us sort through any of our problems whenever we feel stuck, even if those troubles seem as big as elephants. Therefore, we invite you to give yourself a chance to see what you might not have noticed before; approach all that emerges with curiosity. The fact that you are reading this book suggests that you are responding to the longing of your heart and mind, which opens the gateway to seeing what has been obscured.

What if we were to tell you that the actual difficulties that arise in relationships are the ticket to freedom and happiness? Then resisting difficulties would not make any sense at all. Our concept that something is difficult and unsolvable solidifies it. When we simply change our frame of reference from difficult to solvable, significant bindings loosen. We see with fresh eyes.

We assume we are truly correct in how we see things. The part of the mind that interprets our relationship lays claim to it being the way we experience it. The more we are attached to our meaning, the harder it is for us to navigate the situation, much less influence change. Our power lies in remembering that our mind has the ability to create our world. Therefore, our viewpoint and attitudes affect everything.

Dr. Terry Warner states, *The world we respond to and our response to it are one. We choose by our response whether the world will address us invitingly or threaten us menacingly. Herein lies our freedom from fear, anxiety, cynicism, and selfishness: Nothing can harm us emotionally, fundamentally, if we let the truth, especially the truth about the interior life of others, ... write itself upon our souls.*

What does it mean: *The world we respond to and our response to it are one?* It is bold and revolutionary to think in this way. In each interaction we forge either freedom or apprehension. We determine the quality of our relationships: what we put in and what we get out are the same. (If we put an apple pie in the oven, it is silly to think we will take a peach pie out.) Dr. Warner truly challenges us to question our beliefs about what we see.

Repeatedly throughout a day, we are choosing how to see and how to interpret what we see. What we decide is our version of what is. And our version determines how we respond. Viewing the world or each person as we do, already shapes our response and simultaneously creates connection or fear and anxiety.

You have probably heard the story of the man and his unruly children riding the bus. *The man did nothing to stop their behavior. Eventually he said quietly, "We've just come from their mother's funeral. We're all at a loss. We don't know what to do." Suddenly everyone who had been judging both the man and the children saw with new eyes, with compassion instead of judgment.*

How we see people, how we regard them, creates our response.

The Talmud tells us: ***We do not see things as they are, we see them as we are.*** This actuality is why we have to be crystal clear about how we want to be with the people in our lives. Otherwise that untrained Great Dane will be in charge the moment we feel disrespected, hurt, jealous, upstaged, scared, frustrated, ignored, resentful, inadequate, or annoyed... you get the picture.

Notice feelings as they arise, be kind to yourself and understand that this is a moment of choice. You might take the familiar route into the depths of feelings and their subsequent thoughts and responses. It may be almost automatic. With kindhearted awareness and practice you could choose the lionhearted route to freedom.

Happiness blossoms when you relinquish your stories and reconnect heart to heart.

At the moment of impact and each time a replay button is pushed, it is crucial to hold on tight to your intention, to be accountable to your heart's longing for connection, to be responsible for taming your mind. When depleting feelings arise, you can't forget that what is causing your distress is a function of your own thoughts and responses. You cannot permit the Great Dane to overpower the magic of your heart.

We need to cling to our intention; it compels us to be all that we can be in relationships.

Freedom and happiness will only occur when our heart is responding to other peoples' hearts. Dr. Warner tells us we need to let ... *the truth about the interior life of others, write itself upon our souls.* In this statement, he is charging us to experience the heart of the other person.

So, what gets in the way?

NANCY: *I'm too busy for all this nonsense. Why don't people spend time and energy doing the important things, like I do? They are lazy, wasting their lives and my time.*

SHARON: *Kathy calls me every night at my bedtime. I've asked her not to. So now when she calls I think -- Did she forget? Is it an emergency? I wouldn't do this to her. I deserve to have peaceful sleep.*

NANCY: *My colleague got angry with me on Thursday. I squirmed about it. Then I thought -- Well, I am okay now, I understand my weakness and what I need to be and do. It's time for him to move on.*

SHARON: *Truthfully, there are people I have shoved aside, sometimes just putting them out of my mind. I haven't the time or the focus; they are low on my list of what is relevant.*

These quick examples are filled with self-absorption and self-importance. How could we ever see others' hearts with all these indictments and rationale? We hear or see that others are or aren't doing certain things; it is the following steps we take that cause trouble. We take what we see, then rush to judgment based on the meaning we give it from our database. We vote on how others meet our value criteria. It happens unconsciously and automatically. But, what if we are wrong? What if we could be open, flexible, and hold good opinions of people no matter what? What might we see then?

It is who we are being and how we are viewing ourselves and others that shape and give contour to our relationships.

To improve our relationships, we have to develop honest "self-examination." It is easy to look outside ourselves, to point our finger at the other person, accusing them of causing the problem, wanting them to change. Self-examination captures those moments we have been noticing and helps us discern our involvement. From this vantage point, we can start softening, and begin to ask ourselves some probing questions and listen to the responses from our hearts.

- ❖ How might I be a problem for others?
- ❖ How might I not be willing to see them and their concerns?
- ❖ How am I not caring for the well-being of my relationships?

Honestly questioning ourselves, with a sense of curious reflection, can reveal what has been hidden from our sight. Our manner of engaging with people, our side of the equation, has impact.

NANCY: *One day, while sitting alone in a restaurant, waiting for my lunch to arrive, I aimlessly looked around. My gaze fell on a woman facing me some distance away. She looked so mean, like she was angry with me. I couldn't fathom how this stranger could be so unpleasant. I hadn't done anything; her gaze was intensely unfriendly. I was disturbed and felt a little indignant. As I looked away, I saw her get up to go to the restroom. In my mind, I tried to figure out what just happened.*

When the waitress brought my food, I felt my spirits lift in response to her fun exchange and sincere thoughtfulness. As I sat there enjoying my meal, I wondered about the difference of those two states, before and after the food arrived. They were so diametrically opposed, yet sitting so close to each other, side by side. I looked and questioned myself about what previously seemed true.

What I discovered was that when I arrived at the restaurant, there was something lurking undetected inside me. It seems I was stuck in a serious, stern mood, critical and negative about several situations that had occurred earlier that day. My mind was like putty, formed by previous thoughts and experiences. Unknowingly, I carried that contracted way of seeing the world into the restaurant. That mind-space kept me separated from tranquility and serenity in my heart. That is the one who looked at the woman.

The experience Nancy had of the woman was more a reflection of her own inner state than it was of the look on the lady's face. Nancy wanted to believe she was innocent. She was blind to her own inner condition, not seeing what was in her own mind and heart. Without knowing it, she was the one who was inwardly unsociable. In her blindness, Nancy was the architect of her own experience.

From an internal, out-of-sorts stance, she unconsciously searched out and rested her eyes on something that matched her inner state, as if her inner state needed validation. Hunting for something that resonated, Nancy became a human tuning fork. She felt innocent; it was easy to blame someone else. The woman was reflecting back to Nancy her own unpleasantness. Nancy's mind had never lost the capacity to perceive goodness, freedom and happiness. Nor had she lost the ability to be anchored in her heart. However, she didn't have access to them from her contracted attitude and disturbed state.

It is good to pause here and wonder how much is happening in our own lives because of the energy we are projecting out into the world. Are we as innocent as we would like to believe? Do we want to continue to operate as if we were still on the playground at recess time, punching back, not letting someone play, grabbing the ball, or pulling hair to get our way? *Jimmy is being mean to me. Susie's not sharing.* We've grown and hopefully matured. If we are still blaming others, nothing much has changed.

It might seem easier not to take responsibility; although hiding the truth creates another level of unhappiness. Waiting for others to change is a losing game. Furthermore, claiming innocence is laden with blame and distances us in relationship. We don't want to blame ourselves either.

Blaming ourselves or others is deceptive, evasive and destructive.

Blame and innocence draw us away from truth and separate us from people. Instead, we need to be clear and honest with ourselves. We need to put both blame and arguments for our innocence down once and for all and plant ourselves in the magic of oneness.

It is time to use the wisdom available to us from our heart-mind connection.

Wisdom is the result of honest introspection. It's a little humorous to think that on any given day, we have wildly different outlooks, feelings, and interactions. They arise directly from our own perceptions and attachments to ideas. In order to draw the best conclusion we need to be more aware moment to moment: of our assessments, our judgments, and stories we create and claim as "truth." Noticing in this way will help us cultivate awareness of how we are being in our own hearts. Claiming innocence is a copout.

> NANCY: *As the woman I had judged to be mean and angry was leaving the restaurant with her lunch companion, I glanced towards her and smiled and received a friendly smile in return. For a few more days I kept thinking about my restaurant experience. It felt as if it was a thumbnail sketch of my life. I began to wonder about myself and how I had been missing out because of the way*

I was walking around in my world. I became more aware of times when a somber stance seemed rather normal and quite familiar inside myself. I also wondered how this outlook had affected people and situations.

The actual difficulties that arise in our relationships are the ticket to freedom and happiness.

Even though Nancy doesn't have an ongoing relationship with the woman at the restaurant, that experience opened the window on what she needed to see in her mind's concealed, unexcavated world. Typically, the closer or more important the relationships are in our lives, the more searing the reflection is to us. What each of us sees in others that we don't like is reflecting what needs to change in ourselves in order to live more fully from a happy heart. Those reflections are the catalysts that reveal what has been hidden. Just beneath what we don't like is a person. Love pulsates in their heart and beckons our heart to respond.

Uncomfortable exchanges are important moments reminding us to be the witness and to examine how we perceive the world around us. We need to slow down not only our thoughts, but our breath (slowing to a relaxed turtle-pace,) to observe the state of our own mind. Bringing our heart-mind, our state, back to balance is taking responsibility for our behavior in and impact on the world. By coming to peace with the people that occupy our heart and mind, we liberate ourselves and simultaneously offer them freedom.

We are always an influence; how we influence is a choice we make. Remember this fact from the perspective of science in the Heart chapter: hearts have the capacity to change physical matter. The condition of our hearts can be felt by others and has an effect on them. Our inner stance either pleases or offends. It defines the space between hearts.

We have a better chance that our life will go well when we are more interested in solving the issue than in being self-absorbed, making ourselves right, and focusing on our pain or what we deserve. We will be able to see everything more clearly. From a balanced heart-mind perspective, we approach the world very differently. Viktor Frankl said,

Everything can be taken from a man or a woman but one thing: the last of human freedoms -- to choose one's attitude in any given set of circumstances, to choose one's own way. His life provides an eloquent example.

One more point about Nancy's story. The state of friendliness and good humor offered by her waitress shifted Nancy's heart to a more open, receptive, peaceful state, allowing her to consider the situation carefully. This is similar to when Sharon was angry with Roger as she was driving in the snow storm. Noticing the beauty of the snow opened up lightness in her.

Peace of mind is a choice. Invitations abound. Our job is to receive their magic and allow our hearts to release back into love.

Moments of peace and joy are already embedded in our hearts. We have memories of meaningful relationships with friends, family and co-workers.

- ❖ What is your experience of the wonderful people you know?
- ❖ How do you feel in their presence?
- ❖ Even just thinking of them, what do you feel: appreciation, respect, compassion, or oneness?
- ❖ In what ways do they light up your life?
- ❖ Spend a few moments being grateful for having them as friends.
- ❖ Can you feel your heart growing brighter?

In the chapter titled Heart, you brought to mind many moments in your life that generate a joyful, loving heart. Go and revisit those spaces of music, nature, and other uplifting activities now. Connect to their expansive energy. Let yourself bask in buoyant memories of friends and experiences in your life. Feel your heart expand, soften, even smile.

Next, bring to mind one of your relationships that is troubled, but isn't too difficult for you to look at. Don't pick the most horrible, awful, no-good relationship. Freeing our hearts in a less difficult struggle can give us confidence and leverage for the more entrenched ones.

Hold onto the receptive, loving energy that you've established. It is truly who you are and how you want to live your life. Own it completely as you begin to self-reflect on your heart-mind stance in this relationship. Take time to uncover genuineness. With gentleness, ask yourself:

- ❖ What am I bringing to this relationship that I need to take responsibility for?
- ❖ How am I part of the problem?
- ❖ To what am I clinging?
- ❖ How am I holding back?
- ❖ How am I perhaps refusing to be helpful to the person?
- ❖ Is this person really intending to be offensive? Even if they are, do I have to take offense?
- ❖ What is their need?
- ❖ What might be their struggle?
- ❖ What is their heart inviting me to see?
- ❖ What fuel have I thrown on their suffering?
- ❖ What do people who love them see, that I am missing?
- ❖ How might those faults I blame them for show up in me?
- ❖ How does that keep me from seeing them or their good intent?
- ❖ How would love respond? What is my heart whispering and needing me to hear?
- ❖ What simple kindness does my heart want to offer?
- ❖ How do I resolve to be with this person, as we go forward?

Remember what Mother Teresa said: *It is not what we do; it is how much love we put in the doing. It is not what we give; it is how much love we put in the giving.*

Imagine True Forgiveness opening a door
for you to walk through --
takes your hand, welcomes you with reverence
to see anew a moment of
disappointment and separateness
from another.

Like the confluence of two rivers,
allow mercy and sincerity
to merge;
expand your vision,
becoming kindhearted, tender,
expressing only love and respect.

Because you have been doing the exercises and deeply pondering many questions thus far, you have been welcoming yourself to your heart, more and more, recapturing oneness. Let's return to Dr. Terry Warner's quotation, *The world we respond to and our response to it are one. We choose by our response whether the world will address us invitingly or threaten us menacingly. Herein lies our freedom from fear, anxiety, cynicism, and selfishness: Nothing can harm us emotionally, fundamentally, if we let the truth, especially the truth about the interior life of others, write itself upon our souls.*

We cannot be truly happy unless we are invested in other people's happiness as well.

Breathe easily. Seeing with clearer vision actually sets us free.

Give yourself space to feel goodness not only in other's hearts, but in *your* heart as well. Your choice is to perceive goodness and respond appropriately from your heart to theirs.

Perhaps you need to ponder your relationship further. Take the time you need to contemplate. Have no worries. Lean in fully to Dr. Warner's words. Freedom and happiness rest in his promise.

BREATHE

Relax. Inhale... Exhale

BREATHE

In the lovely fable told by Carol Lynn Pearson in her book *The Lesson*, we meet Robert in first grade needing to work through a problem. As he matures, each problem acutely tests his abilities. His teacher is always kind and patient, giving Robert reassurance and encouragement. Now elderly, still having problems to solve, Robert realizes... *that all the problems he had been working on all his life had really been only one problem—this problem: "Robert, how much do you love?"*

Lucky Robert. Lucky us. Breathe easefully; softly and gently, allow yourself to rest in the fullness of your own heart. Refresh your resolve for your intention. Hold it inside, then consider Robert's question:

How much do you love?

What does it mean to love? Robert certainly turns our usual questions -- "How much do you love *me*?" or "What am *I* getting and what's in it for *me*?" -- upside down. The answer to his penetrating question might be best answered by another question. How often do you make the choice for respect, tolerance, trust, generosity, understanding, and good will? Only you know how you have treasured others, how you have been supportive, how you have been able to forgive.

The love and happiness we experience are the fruits we enjoy from choices we make. Strengthening our heart-mind connection makes us better at loving others. This heart-mind partnership enhances every aspect of our lives. Refining it is worth our effort.

Here are some stories from our clients. Taking one step at a time they each journeyed to more peace-filled, loving moments and relationships. You are in good company.

Simone finds how tender life is when your heart is open to others.

> *I've been practicing seeing and caring more for the people around me. Last week I went to Trader Joe's with my children. I needed to buy olive oil.*
>
> *An old man, who was almost invisible, was standing by the olive oil shelf. I stood close to him. I heard him say something. Instead of saying in my mind: What's this guy doing? I can't be bothered; I'm busy, I said, "What did you say?"*
>
> *He said ever so slightly, "I am having a stroke; I cannot move; call 911."*
>
> *My heart swells at this opportunity for being human.*
>
> *Yes, I got him help; stood by him until someone else could help. My kids were pretty much oblivious because they were near the tasting station.*

Charles rides an emotional roller coaster before becoming happy.

> *I got demoted from being president of the company. I was angry and fuming with pride. I had worked so hard and I was agonizing over swallowing my failure and embarrassment. I had never failed before.*
>
> *After those initial emotional heaves and pains, I knew I wanted to be successful. I realized happiness did not come from being the "Big Guy," something that I had only fooled myself into thinking I was. I took steps I needed to take as a beginner. First step was patience. Second, humility.*
>
> *I started becoming happier as I began rebuilding relationships with people. I saw I was much more suited for the new position. I could help the company more from here, and actually deliver what they had hoped for from me as president.*

Ginny has new insights about her mom.

I took a journey to the core of my anger, my resentment, and my inability to see the humanity of my Mum. I had wanted to be better than her, to change her, and to protect everyone from what I saw as the faults in her. I regretted how I had hurt her.

On Tuesday evening I phoned my mum and asked her out to dinner. My mum LOVES good food, and I sensed she would love time with me. I never gave her any time alone with me. I said this treat was a thank you meal for the unconditional love she has given me through all the years. I asked her to wear her favourite dress and said I would wear a dress too. It has always brought her happiness to see me in a dress and I have NEVER -- other than on my wedding day -- worn one on any occasion with her, probably out of spite.

She chose her favourite restaurant and I cannot tell you how amazingly childlike and excited she was. And what was amazing, so was I. She was going to come and help me bathe and put my boys to bed, and then we would get ready together and go out. Never in our entire lives have we done anything like that; I avoided mother-daughter events like the plague.

Last night we had our dinner. We had a glorious meal, and I listened. She brought photos of my childhood, holidays, cakes we made, fun times. Times I had blocked out. We laughed a lot, we smiled and we giggled. What was most amazing was as I listened and truly heard her, I liked her; she is fun!

She came alive in front of my eyes, a little girl who had been asking to be seen and heard glowed with excitement. And do you know what? So did I. I saw my mum in her wholeness, her listened to, loved, heard self, and she is beautiful, truly beautiful, a little girl full of joy, a woman who has joy in her heart. I can see her.

Today my mum came to play with my boys and me, and I let

> *her be with them without judgment or protection. The three of them laughed and giggled together like three little kids. It was amazing... I can see my mum, and she is beautiful....*

Christopher has soft, new eyes.

> *I saw a man on campus that I have seen in a class before. In the past I had thought of him as a dork and I had heard fellow students say uncomplimentary things about him. As I walked down the hall I had a vision in my mind's eye of him as real and human as myself, not a dork, or weird, or worthy of criticism or ridicule, but just a person. At that point I felt compassion for him, not pity, just compassion as a fellow traveler on this journey. I realized at that moment how freeing and uplifting it can be to see people in this way.*

Jerry connects with his son.

> *Daren is our third of four children, our first son. I have a tendency to be a bit tough on him and tend to correct instead of building our relationship. I picked Daren up from baseball practice on Saturday and we went and got a Slurpee. We proceeded to walk near our home and I asked Daren what he liked best about himself. His first answer, "I like being tall."*
>
> *I asked what characteristics about his personality did he like? He said, "Being nice, smart, kind to others, a good brother." I agreed with all his assessments and gave him even more. I let him know that Dads can make mistakes too. I let him know about times where I wished I had been more patient, more present with him, and just nicer. He laughed and said I was still an awesome dad. We then started throwing the baseball back and forth on a beautiful, sunny Saturday afternoon and the world felt wonderful.*

Walid becomes brave.

> *The person I became in our marriage was selfish. My wife deserves to belong and be a part of my present. My*

contemplation was heavy and I was loaded with anxiety. Could I step closer to her? How can this luggage that I've carried be dropped so easily after embracing it so long ... my arms are used to it now. I thought: can I simply unclench my hands and let go?

Then I thought about what I constantly ask for... peace.

So, I walked over to my wife who was in the living room using her laptop. I wrapped my arms around her and this is what I said: "There have been times when I wanted to be with you in a certain way, but I didn't act. How about tonight I cook Chinese noodles, and we just sit and talk about us?"

In that discussion we talked about getting our lives back. We talked about setting up the backyard for candlelight dinners and quiet evenings.

Scary, unfamiliar, uncomfortable, but as we continued our talk it became a feeling of better than great!

Masha discovers the love she has been wanting.

I use to complain that my husband never talked to me. He is so quiet, I didn't even know if he loved me and that hurt. I became aware that I needed to think about him more than focus on what I wasn't getting.

Here is what came to me: He's kind and thoughtful, and he'll do anything for me. He always remembers to do what he says he'll do, like pick up Samuel after school or buy something at the store. He can make anything, and if he sees I need something, he makes it for me, like a bookshelf he made and a place for boots outside our door. And he collected scrap lumber and built us a beautiful new dining room table with an inlaid design. When he gets paid, he gives me all the money ... he doesn't even save any out for himself.

Making this list I saw how amazing he is and began laughing at myself and the hurt I was carrying. I realized that maybe he talks in actions and I just haven't been listening right. I'm really lucky. And I actually FEEL his love, so maybe he doesn't need to talk more.

Sharon wakes up.

My daughter, Lisa, called one night. We live at opposite ends of the country. She told me her babysitter wasn't going to be able to come anymore because she'd lost her driver's license. Lisa has three kids and works full time. The following week was spring break, so the kids would be off school. She said, "I wish you were the kind of grandma who lived down the street and didn't work." I laughed and said, "Yeah, I do too." And we went on to talk about other things.

That night I woke up and sat bolt upright and said, "I want to go help her." It was such a strong sense; I've never felt anything like it. It took a lot of arranging... I had to cancel a workshop that I was scheduled to do for a company, and reschedule clients. But it seemed fairly easy to do; I was so clear. Lisa couldn't believe I was doing this, it seemed so unlike me. I went and had such a wonderful time. I got more time with the kids than usual because they were so available to do fun things. And my heart felt very open to Lisa.

Toward the end of my stay she asked me if I'd consider meeting her in Washington, D.C. to attend a conference. I was thrilled, and said, "YES." We roomed together in a hotel and attended some sessions together, and some separately, and had a truly memorable time. I remember us walking down Connecticut Avenue arm in arm. The amazing thing was that I had always thought Lisa was critical of me. During that time, she wasn't critical once. BUT I found myself biting my tongue several times, about to say critical things of her. Imagine my amazement. I was so wrong about who she was.

Kristy is surprised in this moment.

A few weeks back, after a late flight, I was picking up a rental car from a man who seemed weary and harried. With a long line of people waiting to be helped, it was easy to sense the impatience, or the mere potential for it. When I got to the counter, I did what I normally wouldn't -- asked him how he was -- and commented he must be feeling like he needed a break. He smiled instantly and all the impatience in the air went away. He helped me quickly and efficiently and joked with me in a way that made my own late night feel so much better, less of a burden and more full of possibilities. It was such an unexpected and unique conversation that was carried out so simply.

Joe is amazed to discover what works.

I have worked for this same global company for thirty-one years, mostly on the executive team. They seem to value me, even though I'm the only person on the team without a college degree. They send me wherever in the world a project is stalled. They say I get focused under pressure. My nickname is "The Bulldog."

They were always happy with my results until the lead man on a project quit the company and said it was because I was "abusive." I was shocked. I thought everyone knew I liked them and just got heavy to get things done. We always went out for hamburgers together at the end of the day and I thought we were friends.

So my company president said I'd have to change my approach, if I wanted to keep my job. In coaching, I learned that when I get too intense, I turn into my dad, who was a yeller. I yell and call people names. It was automatic. I thought it was the only way to get things done. I realized that I really cared for these guys and had not shown that in any way except paying for their dinners. It was the only way I knew.

Gradually I saw how it must feel to work for me. I was ashamed. Although I'm tough on the outside, I'm actually soft on the inside. I started to let that part of me show a little. I started thinking of myself more like a sheep dog than a bulldog.

I started listening. I'd gather the key people on a project when I got there, and ask them what was going on. When I'd go off in my mind to "fix" a problem, I'd remind myself to stop and listen: "Pay attention to what these people have to say. They actually know more about this project than you do. There's no need to prove yourself and be the hero, especially if you leave dead bodies on the road." I also got interested in how I could help people learn and grow.

To my amazement, this new approach worked! We got results. People were a lot happier. And so was I. It's actually lonely being a yeller. The clincher was when my wife, Ruby, told me I'd become a lot easier to live with!

Judah recaptures his heart.

I had been in a marriage that had become a business-like partnership rather than a loving union. I continually blamed and accused Rachel of unloving attitudes, for which I alone was guilty. I had in fact invited and encouraged her to withdraw love and shield herself. She found safety behind a self-defensive wall. As I looked carefully at what I had done, I realized that my refusal to love her, or to accept her love as it was offered, had terribly wounded her. Rachel deserved far better, and I was ashamed. So, I felt that it was time to lay out this new understanding before her, and to ask her for forgiveness.

Although I felt a bit nervous, I asked Rachel to sit down with me so that we could have a talk. I began by telling her how I realized -- despite all of my past craziness -- how much I loved her, how much regret I had, and how deeply sorry I was for the hurt that I had caused her. I asked her to forgive me. To see the look in her eyes, as they first widened in surprise and then slowly softened, brought tears to my eyes. After a minute or so of silence, she quietly said that I had never, in over twenty-four years, talked to her in this way, and she was astonished.

We then alternated talking about our vision of what we wanted our relationship to be. Interestingly, there was zero conflict between us. Instead, we found ourselves in one-hundred percent agreement about the quality and nature of relationship that we both wanted. The hug when we finished our conversation was the best ever (!) ... and our interactions since then have been gentle, playful and loving. I noticed that she dressed up differently for work the next morning, in clothes that really highlighted how beautiful she is. When I told her how cute she was, she just looked at me and grinned.

Clearly, it's much better when how we are with one another comes from our hearts rather than our heads.

Alma becomes present.

Reading time with my son typically goes like my life goes: Read for ten minutes just to get it done, kiss him on the cheek, tell him I love him, tuck him in and check it off the list. Doesn't that sound so sad? It has been almost a chore for me. I couldn't finish fast enough so I could get back to whatever I was doing that was so important.

So! I changed my mindset and decided to TRY "staying on task" during reading time with Lenny. Being in the moment. Actually BEING there with him, in the book, in the PRESENT.

The difference. The absolute difference: stories we have read before came to life. He was laughing more, we were imagining more, we read a few extra pages together.

His whole energy has been noticeably brighter in the last few days. I like to think it's partly because of this simple change, even during something as seemingly simple as reading time. And what I find most interesting about the whole thing is that he did not do ONE thing differently, I DID. My actions affect him. My choices affect him. He can feel my rush. He can feel when I'm not there. He can sense if my heart and mind are elsewhere.

These moments and anecdotes are from people just like us, choosing to answer their hearts' whispers. It takes courage and commitment to drop all the stories that keep us from fulfilling our longing for connection. We need to become lionhearted. The reward is amazing. If the people whose stories you just read were asked Robert's question: "How much do you love?" their answer would be: *more than I could have imagined.*

There is nothing more precious for both parties than honoring the pulsation of love connecting hearts. Those words might seem strange when describing a business relationship, but "honoring the pulsation of love connecting hearts" is exactly what happens when two people collaborate effectively, or when one person helps the other succeed.

How do these stories inspire you? Are fresh possibilities dawning on you? Do they help you return to what your heart wants most?

The next chapters will give you more understanding, counsel and inspiration to step further.

TROUBLE

Make Sincere Efforts To Improve

TROUBLE

SHARON: *Sitting at the airport people watching, I saw two airport personnel talking animatedly. I couldn't hear their words, but I could hear the cadences. They were complaining about someone. They both frowned, looked angry, then laughed. The man moved away, coming in my direction. Suddenly the woman ran toward him, grabbed his arm and said, "I forgot to tell you the best part! You'll never believe what he said...." They walked off together, continuing the rise and fall of their shared secrets.*

In this book, we've been encouraging joyful ways to connect with others' hearts. And yet we run into trouble with so many thoughts and tendencies. They are all human, like the gossiping in Sharon's airport story.

Unconscious chitchat and unkind remarks and gestures are so common that we usually don't even notice them. At work, in meetings, around family, they come automatically. They pour through our minds, fall from our lips, or roll our eyes as naturally as waterfalls cascade off a mountain ridge. They are our habits. In our culture they are the norm. It is a way we bond with one another.

Gossip in a family can tear it down and rip it apart.

The rumor mill in an organization can bring it to its knees and destroy it.

Bringing up others' misdeeds or our suffering, hurt and innocence invites others' sympathy or cajoles them to join us in our misery. Conspiring, we now have a buddy, someone who understands our pain. We even run out to get more evidence, more cheerleaders to gather around us. Lo and behold, we begin to believe what rambles through our thoughts.

> *One day Nasrudin and his friends decided to play a joke on the people in a village. Nasrudin drew a crowd, and lied to them about a gold mine in a certain place. When everybody ran to get their hands on the gold, Nasrudin started running with them. When asked by his friends why he was following them, he said. "So many people believed it, I think it may be true!"*

Our wrong thinking can convince us that it is good to have a confidant, someone we can bare our soul to. On the other hand, look at what we are doing with these aspersions: we are inserting disrespect into everyone's lives; we are spoiling people's good names; we are making ourselves more important; we are ignoring our own faults for the sake of blaming others; we are digging up dirt to make ourselves look clean. Who is doing what wrong? Who has harmed me? Who can I tell? How could we possibly consider this helpful? Yet, we've adopted this way of connecting with others.

When pulling someone else down, our intention and connection to oneness fly out the window; our thoughts are a total distortion. Even though gossip feels satisfying at the time, we lose energy, draining dry the ocean of love. How can we justify that? And honestly, how helpful is it to add salt to wounds? How is it going to increase love in our hearts?

> SHARON: *I attended a week-long meditation retreat in upstate New York. After the first morning, my roommate, Eileen, and I both shared our disappointment in the leader who supposedly had been meditating for years. He seemed a little shallow, we both thought. That evening we talked with Bev, our third roommate. She agreed with us. For two more days, the three of us talked several times a day, sharing our latest evidence that the leader didn't know what he was doing. Our sharing was negative, but we were happy to have found solace with kindred spirits.*

On the third day, as we were talking together, somewhat conspiratorially, Bev suddenly said, "Stop! Let's end this gossiping and complaining right now. It's not helping us get what we came for." Eileen and I were shocked, but we quietly consented.

What courage it took for Bev to change the trajectory of the relationship between the three roommates. She also steered their thinking of the leader and the retreat in a different direction. As a result, other participants in the program could relax more since the threesome's disdain wasn't heavy in the space.

- ❖ Have you noticed yourself having a tendency to complain?
- ❖ Where do you find yourself talking poorly about someone, drawing people into your web of ridicule?
- ❖ How compelling is it for you to join a tongue thrashing of someone?
- ❖ Do you fear you'll be rejected if you don't join in?
- ❖ What would it take for you to care enough about your own heart and others' hearts that you could become as courageous as Bev?
- ❖ Freed from the need to gather injurious evidence, what might you see about the person or people you've been talking about?
- ❖ How could you instead bond in love, caring or helpfulness?

A couple of other things that get us down and keep us from truly seeing others are our expectations, and the "shoulds" we carry around. We make assumptions. Sometimes these come from believing the advertising that bombards us. Sometimes they come from experiences in our past, or strong desires that we have.

SHARON: *I once worked with a young woman named Denise. We had lunch together one Valentine's Day. She was excited because Todd, her long-term boyfriend, had invited her for dinner.*

The next day I asked how it had gone. She said, "Terrible. I think I have to break up with him." I was surprised and asked what had gone wrong. "Well," she said, "He cooked me a delicious dinner. The table looked beautiful, my favorite flowers in a vase, candles lit, music playing. It all seemed very romantic." "So what went wrong?" I asked, incredulous. "That was it," she said. "No engagement ring." I looked puzzled, so she repeated it. "He didn't give me an engagement ring." "So?" I said. "He gave you a wonderful evening. It sounds amazing."

Then I told her that I didn't receive an engagement ring for Valentine's Day. I'd been happily married for many years. She couldn't believe it. "You're kidding," she said. "I thought all guys knew that if you really loved a woman and had an understanding, you HAD to give her an engagement ring for Valentine's Day."

In relationships, expectations create a veil that prevents us from seeing the other person.

All we see is how far they are from the picture we carry in our heads of how they should be. The sad thing is that when we're evaluating someone based on how they compare with who we think they should be, or how they should respond, we are blind to them. Denise almost totally missed Todd's wonderful, joyful dinner, his heart that had gone into the preparation, and the thoughtful, loving care he'd taken.

Adriana and Tam ran into another kind of difficulty.

Adriana drove Tam to her doctor's appointment, and then she went to the museum just down the street. She asked Tam to call her when she was ready to be picked up. The trouble was that Tam had failed to get Adriana's cell phone number, so when she was ready to call, she didn't have the number. She also forgot she had turned her phone off in the doctor's office, since the sign said, "Turn off cell phones." So when Adriana tried to call her, Tam didn't answer. This resulted in a huge disconnect. Tam walked to the museum to find Adriana. It was raining, so she got soaked. She couldn't find Adriana there, so she walked back to the doctor's office and waited, feeling upset with herself for not knowing the number. Tam was not well, so the weather and her worry took an extra toll.

Adriana kept calling, but Tam didn't answer. Her phone was off. Adriana was worried and upset, too. At long last they found each other, but not before they had both spiraled downward into a sense of inadequacy and gloom. They both felt frightened and distraught. Tam didn't sleep that night. The next day Adriana didn't return her calls.

It is hard to know how to recover in a relationship when we make a mistake. Everyone makes mistakes now and then. Sometimes it seems hard to accept human foibles. Instead we feel mad at the other person, accusing them either to their face, or in our heart, for making us feel upset, for doing this to us!

Alternatively, if we carry responsibility and self-blame as burdens or punishment, we may feel guilty, and get down on ourselves. We remember the other mistakes we've made. We may feel incapable of doing anything right. Neither choice solves problems. Unfortunately, we can circle round and round, berating the other person or ourselves, while sinking into misery. We feel stuck, not anchored in our loving heart.

Getting unstuck is achievable. We have to open the conduit of forgiveness in our heart, allowing love to spill out over the thoughts in our mind. This openness alleviates wariness, soothes apprehensions, and dissolves fear with compassion and gentleness. That is the remedy, being compassionate, being kind, and being gentle. Actuating these qualities in moments like Tam and Adriana experienced takes practice. Cultivating these characteristics is similar to filling our savings account with money, so that we can draw from that wealth when we feel stuck again. These elegant attributes support every one of our relationships.

We've mentioned complaining, gossiping, blaming and fault finding. We named expectations, shoulds, assumptions, self-blame and misery. Also, don't take pride and self-interest lightly. They keep us small, even though we adopt them to feel big. They get in the way like quills on a porcupine. They send everyone running.

There are many other ways that serve as wedges lodged in relationships between people. See if you can name a few. They might look small, like annoyance, or more active, like bargaining, keeping score, withholding, or being a martyr. They are recognizable because we would be embarrassed to admit them in public.

All of these ways of feeling separate from others are self-absorbed. They do not help us resolve the issue, feel closer, or move on. They generate only negative energy. These ways of feeling separate are very human. We all do them AND they always create problems in relationships. We need to eliminate unhelpful ways of relating to people. Like Bev, we must stop being careless or permissive, letting ourselves off the hook. Destructive patterns truly inhibit our wonderful heart.

> NANCY: *A client, who is a former heart surgeon, told me about Constrictive Pericarditis, which means there is scar tissue around the heart -- like clamps which are constricting it. An inflammation causes the covering of the heart to become thick and rigid, making it hard for the heart to stretch properly when it beats. As a result, the heart chambers don't fill up with enough blood. This condition prevents the heart muscle from expanding and instead tightens the muscle. A heart surgeon has to do surgery and dissect away the scar tissue that is squeezing the heart.*

Let's think about this heart condition as a metaphor that describes our resistance to -- or defensiveness with -- others. Our dislike of someone or judgment of their behavior tightens up our thoughts and feelings towards them. We are mentally, emotionally squeezing our heart and not allowing it to expand. It is very much like saying, "I don't want to make room for you." We become rigid and inflexible. We tell any story we can to keep this miserable tale alive. We excuse our behavior, often blaming them for causing the pain and heartache we feel.

We are sedated by our wrong thinking and don't even know we are.

It is as if we are in a daze, systematically putting clamps in place one by one, sometimes unconsciously. However, every clamp limits love, joy and spontaneity. We steadily squeeze the life out of our heart and out of relationships.

Often people think they should work on themselves so that they eliminate these things: cut out the drama, the blaming, and the "judging stories" they make up about others. Stop gossiping. Those are good ideas. But even if we're able to stop these things when we're not being triggered, we often fall back into our habits when negative thought patterns are reactivated.

Chloe has been struggling in this way for a long time.

> Chloe thought her daughter-in-law, Michelle, was petty and difficult; she didn't like her very much. Chloe frequently complained about Michelle to her husband and all her friends. But she wanted to see and be close with her little grandchildren, Billy and Danny, so she tried to get along with Michelle. She thought of Michelle as a gatekeeper she had to get past.
>
> Before a visit Chloe would make herself a promise to hold her tongue. She would try to get very calm. She would pray and imagine herself not reacting to what she called "Michelle's Barbs." She would try to grow a thick skin. Then, she would take gifts, and in the car on her way, she would paste on a smile. However, when she got to her daughter-in-law's, she was never able to sustain the calm.
>
> Michelle oftentimes did not come to the door to greet her mother-in-law. Michelle received the gifts in a way that appeared cold to Chloe. Harsh judgments of Michelle flooded back into Chloe's head. Sometimes she got so angry that she left before seeing her grandchildren, growing the hostility in her heart toward Michelle.

Wasn't Chloe's preparation helpful? Of course. However, all of Chloe's preparations fell short of her heart. She tried to change her behavior to cover up the feelings in her heart. It didn't work because change happens within our hearts, and in relationship with people, not in our minds. When we are judging, feeling separate, and warring, we are far away from that delicious experience of oneness. The magic hasn't gone away, just our remembrance of it.

Also, think about this: How do you suppose it felt to Michelle to be seen as a gatekeeper her mother-in-law had to get past? Let's suppose Michelle also worked hard to be calm, in anticipation of seeing Chloe. She wanted her sons to know their grandma. Unless she had a change of heart, Michelle's mask would crumble when she met Chloe's judgment.

The outer world becomes a mirror reflecting back to each of us our inner world.

If we are not sincere or our inner countenance has not shifted, simply changing behavior doesn't work. Changing behavior is not enough to change how we are being received in the relationship. We have to have a change of heart. We have to: *let the truth, especially the truth about the interior life of others, write itself upon our souls.*

When there are difficulties in relationships, we might be like Michelle or Chloe, feeling innocent or attacked. The other person says something, does something, and we react. Impulsively, we may say or do something that we're sorry for later. But, we say, "You made me do that." "You caused me to feel the way I do." The emotions that arise seem real, and they are; we know it is so, because we feel them. They might be surging. We might feel right, even righteous, about having them. However, to believe that someone else causes our feelings makes us victims, totally powerless and without recourse.

When we believe that another has caused us to feel a certain way, we are forgetting who we really are, a person with great ability and capacity. We can develop a strong inner core, a heart-mind balance that keeps us steady and at choice in the moments of our lives.

We are the ones choosing our destiny by how we respond to each and every situation.

We have that much power. It is a redeeming posture from which to operate. It puts us in the driver's seat of our life. If we have chosen to feel negative feelings, ones that disable us or drain us of our energy, we can also choose to feel positive ones, ones that will build relationship rather than isolate and separate us from our heart, another person, or situations. We'll develop this thought a little later.

First, let's look at how feelings arise, if they are not caused by someone else. Feelings are thoughts with energy infused in them. They arise from the identifying function of our mind that relates one thing to another, and chooses how we will be in relationship with those thoughts. We have built up an information bank of what we want and what we don't want in our life. We approach most people and situations from this historical perspective rather than as fresh, new interactions. All that history is lying in a latent state within us, as stories, ready to be of service to us whenever we need its defense, or the evidence it provides.

Once we take responsibility for our thoughts and feelings, our troublesome mental and emotional tendencies can be effectively diminished.

With awareness and practice we can see more clearly and change our story to a life of great vigor and vitality, one that is filled with honesty.

To truly improve relationships, our hearts must be engaged in an expanded, responsive way.

We need to see the truth of the other without prejudice: their pain, their sorrow, their hopes and dreams. Not the story we tell ourselves when we want to be right, nurse a wound, or prove a point. We need to see the person from standing in their shoes, experiencing their heart, questioning our own integrity, seeing more and more of the truth of their being, until we come to a place of genuine caring for them.

Love's magic turns this key. In this process we will also hear the truth about ourselves and how we may have been unjust. This kind of honesty creates trust, harmony and enjoyable relationships. True happiness blossoms when that is what we desire for others and what we create for them. This might be a good time to return to the last exercise in the Resolve chapter to deeply consider another one of your relationships.

Dr. Terry Warner says, *To the degree that we become receptive and responsive to the truth, life will keep instructing us. It will teach us all sorts of fresh things about matters we thought we already understood. This is partly because we will no longer perceive them distortedly. We will be more open to seeing things as they are instead of anxiously twisting them to validate any lies we may be living.* Truth is dynamic and exists in the quiet space between people. It is understood in our hearts.

Genuine relationship is seeing the other person with full appreciation -- all that is good and not so good. Letting our hearts be touched by their humanity, we are changed. We don't evolve in isolation. Change in isolation is only as real as yesterday's dream. We need to see ourselves in the mirror of others. That is when we can notice our responses, our openness, and our stuck-upness. Whether we are the owner of a huge corporation, the parent of a rebellious child, a spouse in a deficient marriage, or an adult caregiver, we need to hold each person in our life benevolently. Only then can we solve the most difficult of situations.

We must see what is being revealed about our own self in the relationship, shifting always into a balanced heart-mind perspective, acting and speaking from oneness.

Imagine Grace afoot winding through roadways and glens,
recognizing, honoring simple needs.

Like draping garlands of love 'round dearest friends,
stay connected to tenderness, affection --
wrapping those cold in warmth,
loving those whose eyes
mirror fear or hopelessness.

Pausing to appreciate others' dignity,
feeding their hearts with sunlit smiles,
reveals heaven on earth --
more joy than you ever give away.

The philosopher, Martin Buber, believed that the way to become whole is to engage in our relationships with others. Buber is best-known for his book *I and Thou*, which he wrote in 1923. It focused on the way humans relate to their world.

Buber's philosophy is described this way: *Rather than truly making ourselves completely available to people, understanding them, sharing totally with them, really talking with them, we observe them or keep part of ourselves outside the moment of relationship. We do so either to protect our vulnerabilities or to get them to respond in some preconceived way, to get something from them.* Buber calls such an interaction "I-It."

It is possible, notes Buber, *to place ourselves completely into a relationship, to truly understand and "be there" with another person, without masks, pretenses, even without words. Such a moment of relating is called "I-Thou."*

Even though Buber's language is a little foreign to our ears, we can fully grasp his meaning. What a beautiful, respectful way to think about living and interacting as equals with the people in our lives.

FREE

Know Yourself. Ponder. Forgive.

FREE

Being the recipient of others' heartfelt kindness is gratifying and oftentimes humbling. Collette is surprised to experience such a moment.

The time of year was late October; the place, Toronto. A cold wind was blowing from Lake Ontario as I slowly walked up Yonge Street. Thin as a scarecrow, I was shivering in the warmest clothing I owned, a denim jacket. I was homeless, hungry, and broke. I was fifteen years old.

I stopped to peer in the window of a clothing store, gazing longingly at the leather jackets and fur coats on display. The gray-haired proprietor came to the door. "Come in," he suggested. I shook my head. What would be the point?

He looked me up and down. "I might have something that would fit you, in the back," he said. "I have more than I can use. Come."

I followed him wordlessly to the back of the store. He pulled several coats out of a pile and held them up to me one by one, measuring the fit with his eyes. "This one, I think." He motioned I should try on a knee-length gray suede coat -- clean and warm.

I was stunned. Was this stranger giving me a leather coat? I slipped it on and showed him that it fit. He nodded, satisfied. I stammered out my thanks. He shrugged.

> *I left the store wearing the coat, warm for the first time in days.*
>
> *That store owner never asked me if I had any money, if I owned a warm coat, if I had anyone looking after me. He took one look at me and knew that I had none of those things, that I was cold, and that he could help.*

Colette's story touches our hearts because we know how it feels to be seen, cared for, and helped. Every human being yearns for recognition and kindness. The store owner's sensitivity and generosity exemplify what it means to honor our oneness as people together on earth.

When we think of others and what their needs may be, we increase our inner strength, peace and compassion. These are not soft, touchy-feely traits. They are full of power, energy, and life-force; able to transform the darkest of situations. So often we slip past one of these moments like we didn't notice. The shopkeeper took action; he saw what was needed and responded.

SHARON: *I hugged Delilah, and she started to cry. Delilah had received an e-mail from her good friend Judith, saying that her mother-in-law died last night and today all of her husband's huge family would be coming to her home for a "meal of consolation." Judith was overwhelmed and needing support. She asked Delilah to come help. Delilah reflexively responded saying that she was sorry she could not come, because she was totally busy.*

Now Delilah, standing with me, realizes what she's done. Delilah knows and loves Judith. She refused her friend; she was busy, and rationalized that she didn't know Judith's 93-year-old mother-in-law. Delilah's own tears were telling her that she'd made a mistake. She began to see that if she went to work, then to Pilates, then to a dentist appointment, she would be totally miserable.

Considering further, Delilah realized that all of her appointments could be postponed, and that none of them was as important as her friendship with Judith. She gradually breathed herself into a calm state and sent Judith another e-mail. "Sorry for that first e-mail. I've come back to my right mind. I'll be there." Delilah was now responding to the whisper in her heart.

When we live from our hearts, we respond.

In our hearts, our thoughts, speech and actions arise from the magic space. Delilah began to feel her love for Judith. If she hadn't listened -- had continued on with her day -- she would have abandoned what was most important in her heart. Listening to that whisper, Delilah became clear.

> SHARON: *Seeing Delilah at the end of her day was a testimony. She felt expanded by her choice to support Judith. She appreciated all of the Jewish rituals that were new to her. She felt the power of Judith's mother-in-law's love as people shared stories. She returned from the event energized and bathed in love. As Delilah shared her experience with me, I felt it too.*

By serving Judith's needs, Delilah experienced love. **There is nothing more potent or life-giving than merging the awareness of our heart-mind's state with action.** It wakes up every cell of our body and ripples out and out into the world.

- ❖ How might you be more present to people making requests of you?
- ❖ How sensitive are you to the needs of others?
- ❖ Are you practicing listening to your heart?
- ❖ What will it take for you to follow its guidance as Delilah did?
- ❖ What heartfelt action do you need to take today?

We are changed when our great hearts are steadily fixed on relatedness to others. This effort reduces self-doubt and fear. Anchored here, we leave behind all the burdens, limitations and defenses that weigh heavily upon us when we are engrossed in me and mine. Delilah's first response to Judith was self-focused. It was a reflexive answer similar to a knee-jerk reaction. After a few moments, she let her friend and her friend's need into her heart. By honoring the relationship, her second e-mail would now be compassionate, whether or not she was able to rearrange her day and help Judith.

The sense of *other* dissolves as we become *more we-focused* and relate to *us* as equally important.

By taking this higher path we understand the concerns and goals of other people in concert with our own. Being in relationship is not an either-or domain. Edward Chambers describes relationship as: ... *not limited and divisive. It is additive and multiplicative, not subtractive and divisive.* We become more together.

We complement others' merit by supporting their great qualities. It is a joyful undertaking. It leaves us feeling flexible, fluid, accepting, and at ease -- not guarded and anxious. Most importantly, we recapture our natural, inborn state of love. We become a shining, heart-mind mirror reflecting light and safety. That great light in our heart shines forth with more brilliant luminosity. Others experience it.

Sonya tells this story:

> *The best way I can describe Camilla is "inspiring." I began taking classes from Camilla nearly five years ago. To this day, every time I leave her class I feel inspired to live into my potential, to be my best self.*
>
> *Camilla is very intelligent and super knowledgeable, yet she never comes across as condescending. Rather, she creates an atmosphere of inviting and encouraging each one of us to be better than we even think we can be. Something about being in her presence makes me want to be better, to do more, to strive harder. She believes in the best part of me and holds up the light, encouraging me to live into it and be my best self.*
>
> *Camilla has had a life full of trials. She has had close to thirty surgeries. Her constant quiet perseverance without complaining is so inspiring. Watching her deal with her trials has strengthened me in enduring mine.*
>
> *She makes me feel like I am the only thing that matters to her at that moment. Camilla makes the world a better place, one person at a time.*

Hearing this description of Camilla, we are drawn to think about the people in our lives who have been a great inspiration to us.

Choose one inspiring person in your life to consider in this moment.

❖ What are their shining qualities?

❖ What is it like to experience this person?

❖ How does being with them increase who you are?

❖ How would the people in your life benefit from knowing this person you've chosen?

❖ How would the people in your life benefit from your being your best self?

Relationship requires that we show up as our best self.

For a while Nasrudin worried about each little mistake he had made in his life. Sometimes he would fret out loud over some minor characteristic flaw he had noticed in himself. His wife tried to console him. "Don't worry so much. After all, nobody's perfect." Nasrudin smiled and shook his head, "Ah, but I'm so close."

Nasrudin was not known for having a humble heart. Yet he believed that no one was better at humility than he was. We can probably never learn humility at Nasrudin's feet. Except, maybe we are not so different from him and need to laugh at our own outrageousness.

❖ What do you hold onto as your best or worst trait? How much pride or energy do you invest in your story?

❖ Are you continually measuring your worth or value against other people?

❖ How many times a day are you discourteous?

❖ How often do you comment on others in small ways, even when it is only in your mind?

Humility, patience, compassion, and sincerity are compelling and generous characteristics that we want to cultivate. They dismantle our arrogance, inferiority, and self-focus, and transform our humanness into a truly beautiful presence. Then we can offer our happiness to every moment.

Sometimes this process of unmasking and being our real selves feels so difficult, as if someone is pulling off our skin and leaving us barefaced. Granted, it is a transparent, naked way to live. However, without our masks and pretense, everyone, including us, is more comfortable and at ease. It is a relief to stop struggling in relationships.

Simply being our natural selves, our energy is well spent. Our words and actions have the power of authenticity. Others experience us as genuine and trustworthy. They no longer have to defend themselves from our insensitive thoughts and misdeeds. Instead our honesty and caring pave the way, making it easier for them to be their best selves, to live from their hearts.

We are never just an individual.

Relationship is not a static energy; it is a dynamic dance of individuals growing in the presence of each other -- each person being influenced by the other. That is why it is so important for us to offer our best self. We have to be courageous enough to be vulnerable with others. We have to let go of being in control or having all the answers. Instead, we must become comfortable with not knowing and being in the presence of the unfolding together.

In the aftermath of Hiroshima and Nagasaki, Einstein spoke out about abandoning competition and embracing cooperation, about not controlling and subjugating people. He rallied around the change that needed to be made in the way of thinking and being with one another. He stated ... *the real problem is in the minds and hearts of man. We will not change the hearts of other men by mechanisms, but by changing our hearts and speaking bravely.*

Einstein offers an amazing concept. We can speak bravely, fearlessly from our heart. What a powerful stance! This kind of communication is without impulsiveness or avoidance. Instead it is replete with interconnection. By changing our hearts, we become the proponents for mutual respect and mutual trust in this world. When our heart-mind is operating from its optimum state, it fosters the best: its real design.

Who we are impacts others.

In that same speech, Einstein said... *we must realize we cannot simultaneously plan for war and peace.* When this understanding is abandoned, relationships are harmed. What if, instead, each one of us committed to peace in our heart? Then, our part of the world, where we have influence, would feel that wave and be able to merge into Morrie's metaphorical ocean.

That state of peace was felt at a memorial service.

> SHARON: *Everyone was telling beautiful stories about Weedie. The last man came forward to share. He got to the microphone and said, "I didn't know Weedie, but I wish I had. All of these stories about her loving ways have made this room feel like I imagine heaven to be. Just imagine if the whole world was like this. It would be such a great place!"*

This man used his time at the microphone to speak truth. Everyone felt the same and was moved. His words not only described energetically what was now present in the room, but also identified the superb power of uplifting words and what they are able to engender.

Words set a tone and create either receptivity and understanding or discord. It is as if they are an extension of our physical form reaching out to touch another. Therefore, a fruitful endeavor is for us to stay connected to our heart in order to discern what would be helpful and what is kind. We will then be conscious of what we wish to say, how we wish to touch another human being. Are we being prudent with our words, sensitive, helpful? Will people feel welcomed, safe?

Words are as precious as gold.

Will our communication uplift others or would compassionate silence be more helpful?

Benevolent silence is a powerful gift we can give another person. A quiet mind oftentimes conveys more than words. It is as if the essence of our heart is being offered. We are in attendance. The person feels respected. When someone needs space, silence offers dignity and grace, allowing the person's inner journey to unfold, certain they will find their way.

We have to listen from the still space within to know what to hear. What if we all grew comfortable sitting in benevolent silence with each other? The harmony of joy would resound everywhere, oneness pulsing from within each heart, creating together a magnificent symphony.

As the recipient, it is profound to receive someone's abiding presence when we are distressed. It is comforting and generative to be able to express our perplexity or grief to a generous listener, one who lets us find our way through the quagmire to peace.

> SHARON: *My second husband, Gene, died quite suddenly. I was distraught. He was my soulmate. My dear friend Tina came to me and said, "Tell me all about Gene and about you and Gene and your love." I wanted desperately to talk about him, and felt people were tiring of hearing me. Tina listened, for a long, long time. Her quiet attention wrapped me in snug affection. I emerged from that experience with so much gratitude, much better able to go on with my life.*

But how do we listen when words are harsh, rude, intense or critical?

Warmheartedly.

The only way that truly works is to have our ears attached to our heart so we can hear what is below the intonation, the choice of words, the emotion, and the emphasis. Hold firmly to the oneness that is present as well. All contracting thoughts need to be out of the way. Don't see the moment as an attack. It is better to see what is being said as something incredibly important to them, thoughts flooding through their speech without being pondered in their heart first. Have compassion; intensity is usually due to some inner pain. Our receptive hearts can hear what our ears by themselves cannot.

> ❖ What does the person really want to convey?
> ❖ Is your heart available so that they know you are with them? How much are you willing to love?

❖ How can you provide safety that invites tranquility to blossom in both hearts?

❖ How can you show them you care?

❖ How can your heart be more vibrant than any negative thoughts that may float through your mind?

❖ Can you be so trustworthy that you can gently intervene?

❖ Can your heart be so peaceful that you can say something difficult that needs to be said, in a way that can be heard?

REMEMBER: In a spirit of mutuality, we can speak bravely, fearlessly from our heart. We take care of both parties equally and simultaneously. That brand of honesty in communication keeps dignity intact for people. We can be synchronously loving and firm. For example: disagreeing while maintaining respectful dialogue, giving a performance review that admonishes while generously supporting growth, or being stress-free while assigning chores to a reluctant family for a housecleaning project.

It is an art to fuse those two qualities. Don't worry; be like a new juggler learning his skill of keeping three balls in the air. With practice, committed to our intention and the experience of oneness, hearing and responding to another person's heart is always possible. One heart harmonizes another heart. We are human tuning forks. Steadiness invites others to find balance. Be fearless and take hold of Mary Burmeister's guidance, *Look until you can HEAR. Listen until you can SEE.*

Everything we discuss in this book takes practice, building strong muscles of compassion, patience, and forgiveness -- all for the sake of regaining the sense of oneness. It is possible to mature and expand both our mind and heart for such an Olympian task.

Suppose for a moment you were going to participate in your favorite Olympic event: What would you have to study? How much would you have to practice? What would you have to let go of? What kind of diet would you need to put yourself on? What are the restrictions your trainer would enforce? To what vital self-talk would you have to commit? What would be your daily schedule? Who would be on your support team?

How do you think Michael Phelps won 22 medals?

Isn't happiness your Olympic event?

How compelling is your desire for happiness? The gold medals are yours once you start loving other people's hearts more than being upset. However, you won't display any medals because you will simultaneously know that doing the right thing is not an achievement. It is an integral part of every healthy relationship.

OLYMPIC PREPAREDNESS

Commit.

Step closer to people.

Daily refresh your intention.

Retreat often; rest inside in stillness.

Honor each heart. Return to oneness.

Witness your mind. Make it your friend.

Choose your heart's whispers over your mind's stories.

Be grateful for people who expand your capacity to love.

Tune in to others. Kindly offer support.

Make sincere efforts to improve.

Know yourself. Ponder. Forgive.

Practice. Practice. Practice.

Breathe easily.

NANCY: *I had been thinking about forgiveness and how it can change everything. This is a story my grandson, Ben, shared with me.*

Under Iranian law, a victim's family chooses to show mercy or have an active part in the execution of the accused.

Both families were at a public execution site. The 19-year-old, black-hooded Balal, waited with a noose around his neck. He cried and begged for forgiveness. The victim's mother stepped forward and slapped his face. The two mothers held each other and wept. The victim's parents then removed the noose from Balal. Their change of heart came after a dream where their son told them not to seek retaliation. By freeing Balal, they became free.

Balal is now encouraging his friends not to carry knives, and wishes someone would have slapped him when he carried one.

All of us want the very same things: love, forgiveness and acceptance. Have we become free enough in our own hearts to offer freedom to others? Life is too short and too precious to hold onto negative emotions or stories. It is time to forgive and ask for forgiveness. It is time to be generous, to create paradise here in our own homes, in our communities and at work.

Breathe easily, our friends.

We call you friends since we have walked together on this ambitious journey. We understand what it takes. We are committed to your success. Refresh your intention daily. And breathe freely. Our fabulous breath provides a priceless bridge. It attunes our mind, body and heart. Notice how when you are anxious, the breath quickens and shortens. The opposite is also true. We can dismantle high emotion by breathing life in deeply, all the way to our hearts. Therefore, together let's honor the power of breath.

Consciously fill your entire lungs with breath. Exhale slowly. This will begin to bring you into balance.

Please continue breathing deeply and slowly. Watch how deep, rhythmic breathing calms your mind and establishes you in your body, in the present moment.

Inhale deeply; exhale fully, each exhalation carrying away debris from your mind. Continue breathing with this awareness.

Taking your breath into a yet subtler dimension, imagine you are actually breathing into your heart, expanding it on each inhalation. As your heart becomes saturated with more breath, allow peaceful feelings to surface.

Experience your mind becoming more attuned to benevolence increasing in your heart ... each breath connecting you more to what really matters.

Breathing revitalizes you. Rest in peace and serenity. Breath is your life-line.

You know how to be in relationship. Trust that. Live from your happy heart. Translate what you know to other relationships. Proceed from wherever you are, continually stepping towards the people in your life.

All our relationships have posed this one question -- How much do you love? Are there relationships where you need to stretch a little more, forgive a little more, love a little more? Trust the unfolding of love; it knows the way. With great affection, we thank you from the bottom of our hearts.

May nature's purity and beauty continuously
illumine the silent path to your heart.

May the faithfulness of your inhalation and exhalation
sustain the light of your intention.

May your mind merge into limitless love,
deep compassion,
tender forgiveness.

May laughter and awareness be your constant companions.

And may you walk with grace and serenity
upon this earth
being a blessing to all.

AFTERWORD

We are grateful to have had this opportunity to think about you and all the relationships that you care about. Thank you for being present in our lives and inviting us time and again to take up the pen. The time was right.

Thank you for creating more peace in the world, one relationship at a time. We have walked with you on a sacred path of building respect, compassion, and heart-mind balance in order to be your best self with others. This path is a full circle returning you back to your innate state, to the delightful, happy heart that you truly are.

Whenever you feel lost, don't be afraid. Connect with one of the exercises. Reread the stories in the Breathe chapter. Or become aware of your breath and allow it to carry you back to your heart. The breath is with you wherever you go. You don't have to wait until you get home, or have enough money, or get to a store. Wherever you are, just pause; notice, slow down, and deepen your incredible gift of breath. Let it help you dissolve the thoughts and fears in your mind and usher you back into your heart and body.

Another unbeatable aid is gratitude. Sweet gratitude is one fantastic remedy for any misery. Stepping into a grateful heart mysteriously turns night into day. Keep this healing balm with you always. If things aren't going well, pause (obviously a good help in itself), and begin experiencing gratitude.

If you feel past hope, or too far away from your heart, you can start with gratefulness for your eyes, ears, toes, hands, or any body part. Think about how you take it for granted. What would life be like without it? Actually allow yourself to be amazed by what it provides for you. Once you are a little more relaxed, start adding the blessings that are in your life; even ones that you might not usually think about. Truly experience your deep appreciation for each one. You cannot be grateful and upset at the same time.

Not enough can be said about regularly recalling happy moments. Such moments are named in the Heart chapter. These moments offer more than just thinking a happy thought; instead they have the potential to shift your vision. They clear away the debris of unhelpful thoughts; you begin to see more clearly and respond more lovingly. Once you feel connected to a soothing experience that is alive for you, let its emotion swell inside you, like a bright balloon coming to life. Practice staying with that expansive state as long as you can. It will give you new lenses. You will be able to look at people and situations with more accuracy and receptivity in your heart.

Additionally, a practice that is very beneficial for increasing happiness is to choose a characteristic that you admire, one that you would like to develop in your life. Ponder it each day. Put it into practice in your interactions; watch it mature inside you day by day, until it becomes natural and permeates your life. This is a wonderful way to stay anchored in your heart.

Also, as much as you can, stay away from thinking in terms of opposites -- descriptive pairs of contrary, contrasting labels, like good and bad, wrong or right, kind or mean, rich or poor, smart or foolish. Comparisons bog us down in suffering. They separate rather than connect individuals. Instead, be content. Know you are good and lovable. You don't need to keep checking it out by comparing yourself with others. Only the mind's trickery believes other people are your measuring rod. Regain the experience of oneness and settle into its magic. Know that the warmth in your own heart is your best measure.

Appreciate! Appreciate! Appreciate! Notice your great good fortune. Be free from feelings of lack; fill with peace and contentment. Be happy; be generous.

Embrace the book's uplifting thoughts and mindsets and make them your own. They will help set you free. In that spirit, we request that you wait to teach and coach this material until you have digested it and become alive to its unfolding within. Then your helpfulness will carry the energy of your own heart.

Stay connected to your heart, until it shines as brightly as the sun and fills the hearts of all the people in your life with warmth, affection and good cheer.

With great love and our blessings, Sharon and Nancy

SHARON EAKES
BCC

NANCY SMYTH
MCC

STUDY GUIDE

HEART-CENTERED
STUDY GUIDE

There is a story about an ancient tribal people that has been attributed to many sources.

These people were nomads, traveling from one terrain to the next finding food and shelter wherever they could. Those who had been blessed to travel with them gained wisdom from their words. At some point in their journey, the nomads simply stopped. When those traveling with them asked why they just arbitrarily pitched their tents and brought their travels to a halt, the response was a simple one, "We stopped so that our souls have time to catch up with us."

There is freedom in experiencing our own heart and soul. That inner landscape is where truth is discovered. Knowing when and how to pause and return to our core takes discernment.

Like sitting in the midst of Stonehenge,
become that still.
Enter the depth of your soul,
patient enough to hear truth unraveling,
unbinding your inner eye to see what you haven't seen.

Dare enough to practice.
Expand beyond clever, witty, and smart,
traveling respectfully to wisdom and truth,
transforming great insights into loving action.

We guarantee great benefits from pausing, pondering, and practicing. To that end, the following extensive study guide is designed for you to use: individually, with your friends, and in Book Club gatherings. Pondering the ideas will deepen understanding and create new perceptions. Ongoing reflection gives time to assimilate what is most significant to you. Writing and sharing with others increases understanding as well. All these forms of study strengthen your resolve to make changes to your relationships. Approach your study and practice rooted in the major tenet of this book: **follow your heart's guidance**.

- ❖ Study either as you finish a chapter and/or complete the book.
- ❖ Use as a stand-alone exploration of one or more relationships.
- ❖ Choose the chapters where you need more help to sharpen your understandings.
- ❖ Focus on just a question or two. It can help set the tone for your day or bring clarity in a meeting.
- ❖ Practice consciously what is most important to you.
- ❖ Allow yourself to shift in the way you see other people.

For Book Clubs, we suggest choosing one or two chapters and having people work through the material beforehand. Then gather together for lively, shared conversation to enhance everyone's learning. A leader could guide the discussion.

Relationships are an ongoing journey, a study for life. Enjoy!

HAPPY!

How do you define happiness?

How happy are you?

Describe what you have usually thought of as the path to happiness.

Without any judgment, begin to notice your customary response modes

    a. to stress

    b. to others

What are the clues (physical, mental, emotional) that let you know you are moving away from happiness?

What are three things that happened today that made you happy?

How much are laughter and lightheartedness part of your day?

How does it feel to remember happy people and events? What's the experience in your body? Your mind? Your heart?

Exercise: For a moment think about a particular person who cares about you and values what is important to you. Perhaps you even feel treasured by this person. Is it a family member or a friend? Think about how you cherish them, their wonderful qualities and how they walk through the world.

Notice how caring for them adds significantly to your life.

Remember a special moment with this person. Where were you? What was taking place? Enjoy that memory.

Notice your experience. Truly let yourself delight in having this person in your life.

   a.   Hold onto those uplifting feelings as you approach your next activity.

   b.   Be consciously aware and choose to step towards others rather than away.

   c.   Allow yourself to choose happiness and to offer happiness.

   d.   How can you more easily respond to the people in your life who care about your happiness?

HEART

What new insights about the heart did you gain from this chapter? How might they serve you?

How is the heart's role in happiness different from what you previously thought?

What is your experience of hearing someone's heart calling to you?

How might you increase the physical care of your heart?

What are delightful experiences that have expanded your heart? Bring them to memory now.

a. What tickles your heart and makes it sing?

b. What music sets you free? What rhythm finds your foot tapping?

c. What movement and activities set you free? Dancing, athletics, sports, yoga, hiking, hobbies, reading, travel, photography?

d. Who are your favorite artists? What do they stir in you? What colors would you love to paint the world?

e. What prayers, blessings, scriptures, books, songs or meditations speak to your soul?

f. What in nature calls to you the loudest? Mountains, wide-open valleys, caves, oceans, rivers, canyons, forests, animals, flowers, trees?

g. In nature what is dear to you?

h. Pets and inspiring stories are great stimuli as well. Which pets and stories do you hold in your heart?

Notice how the world brightens and your energy shifts; your perspective opens and sees beauty, wonder and possibilities. Don't these sentiments feel more like the real you? How can you live more from this space? How can you increase your connection to those stimuli?

Immersed in one of these memories, what is possible for you? Feeling this connected to your heart's rhythm, how might you face the day or a difficult situation? Are you more able to sense other people's hearts?

Exercise: Put aside all the identifying labels and roles that you live; and just breathe the simplicity and wisdom of the phrase "I am" into your whole being a few times...

Relax, exhale slowly and effortlessly. Inhaling, softly say "I am." Stay here for a short while, and again, breathe in the simplicity of "I am" .....

For these next unhurried rounds let your vision and body soften, like turning down the volume. As you breathe, allow "I am" to collect in your heart like precious love notes.

Can you sense your heart's pulsations? You might even imagine your heart as a golden vessel waiting to be filled to overflowing with wonder. If you like, you can close your eyes as you practice.

Taking time to truly rest here for longer periods, you can settle down inside yourself. The mind quiets, creating a softer, spacious state of inner wonder. You are not tethered by thoughts or ideas. It's as if you are entering an expanded, unexplored state not as familiar as your daily routine.

Reflecting on the "I am" exercise:

   a. What would it be like for you to live from a more relaxed, heartfelt space?

   b. How much easier would it be for others to be with you?

   c. What is the relationship with your heart that you want to create and commit to?

   d. What small, specific practice could support that happening?

   e. From this heartfelt space, how might you interact more easily in relationships?

What are the deepest yearnings of your heart? What is your heart whispering to you now?

How might you become open to the reality of being light and love, a pure and powerful energy force?

What are the particular heart-centered qualities that shine in you? How can you help them increase and shine brightly? If you are feeling "not me," "nothing special about me," then think of one or more people you truly admire. The qualities that you see in them are also yours. Acknowledge those qualities in yourself. Wonder how those qualities express in you. What is one specific, small way that you can help your gifts increase and shine brightly?

How can you allow yourself to experience the joy that children experience?

MAGIC

What does the concept of oneness mean to you?

When have you experienced oneness? In nature, music, relationships... Either describe or visualize your experience.

What is your level of contentment? When are you most contented?

Exercise: Relax into your breath, inhaling and exhaling softly with ease. When you are ready, gently bring your awareness to your heart. You might like to place your hand lightly over your heart to increase this awareness. Do you notice or hear its cadence? Take your time.

Now, allow your heart to fill with the radiant light of this Navajo chant:

> This that is beautiful, it shows my way;
> This that is beautiful, it shows my way;
>
> Before me is beautiful, it shows my way;
> Behind me is beautiful, it shows my way;
>
> This that is beautiful, it shows my way;
>
> Above me is beautiful, it shows my way;
> Below me is beautiful, it shows my way;
>
> This that is beautiful, it shows my way;
> This that is beautiful, it shows my way.

Deep inside your heart resides boundless love, splendid power, and vast wisdom. Immerse yourself. Beauty surrounds you and enfolds you in an ocean of serenity. Let all thoughts dissolve into an expansive and luminous silence and enter oneness. Dwell here for a while.

Imagine being given new eyes that can see hearts instead of personalities. What might you see? How do you suppose your own heart might be affected?

What might be the advantages for you being alive to oneness, a space of experiencing "one" heart?

Please bring to your mind a person whom you might be overlooking, a person who longs for you to appreciate them.

a. What lets you know their hunger? Is it something they say? Is their behavior begging for your attention? Could it be a whisper you hear in your heart?

b. What are their great qualities? How have you seen love shine through them?

c. Can you recognize the longing in their heart?

d. In what ways are they more similar to you than different?

e. How have you let them know they are not worthy of your love?

How are you feeling now towards the person who longs for your appreciation? What action do you wish to take?

Who are other people you step away from in your heart? What would it take for you to experience "one" heart with these people?

MIND

How do you experience your mind: friend or foe? How do you know?

What happens to your energy when you are consumed by worry or fear about something in the future?

Do you ever notice the way your mind compares, judges and comments? Pause and ponder these questions:

    a. How do you carry harshness into life?
    b. What is the impact of your judgments?
    c. How might critical thoughts affect your life?
    d. Might others sense your critical mind?
    e. How are others not deserving of your demeaning thoughts?

What do you understand about the statement: The mind creates the world we experience.

How might you take more responsibility for your creations?

What is the general condition of your mind? Wild to tamed: where do you hang out on that continuum? How can you recognize when the Great Dane takes charge?

What gentle self-discipline can you commit to in order to take you off the emotional slippery slope?

What quiets your mind? What slows it down -- breath, connecting to nature, music? Experiment. Get to know what works for you.

What powerful thoughts or images always bring you back to peace?

What stories about yourself or others do you cling to? How do they disturb your mind? How do they create your unhappiness?

CONSCIOUS

What do you notice?

a. How conscious are you of the world you inhabit throughout the day?

b. To what degree are you awake?

c. Did you notice a stranger's smile?

d. Did you see the stars in the sky last night?

e. What color are your friend's eyes?

f. What else might you be missing along the journey?

g. How might you be blind to yourself?

Noticing is an art. It is free of comments or judgments. It simply sees what is. Are you able to open to see with subtle vision: who you are? how you impact others?

Presence, Respect, Deceleration, Openness, Discernment, and Patience help awareness to blossom. Which quality would you like to cultivate to improve your awareness of yourself and the world around you?

Choose the quality that you could commit to; research its meaning and begin implementing it for a week. Notice the way you are approaching life as you develop this quality.

Every minute of every day you have the ability to make choices about what to do and how to do it, what to think and how to think, and literally, how to be with others. What goes into making the choices in your life?

a. Is there thoughtfulness?

b. Is there impulsiveness?

   c. Is there convenience?

   d. Is there desire?

   e. Is there awareness of how choosing will affect you? ...and others?

   f. What are the underlying intentions of your life that influence making a choice? If you don't have a clear intention, how will you know how to choose?

In any given moment, including this moment, we are choosing our response to each situation. What is your choice in this moment?

Become crystal clear about how you want to be with the people in your life. Take time to contemplate each question:

   a. How do you want your relationships to improve? How do you want to be? How will success look and feel?

   b. What will this outlook provide for you?

   c. How will others benefit?

   d. Who are the specific people who will be affected? How will your improvement help them?

   e. What is the internal shift you need to make in order to hold and honor your relationships?

   f. What is an intention that compels you to be all you can be in relationships?

   g. How can this intention be such an irresistible vision, so meaningful to you, that your whole being consents to it?

   h. How can you dedicate yourself to making that happen?

Please become succinct and record your intention.

On a scale of 1-10, how ready are you to live everyday life in an extraordinary way?

What will it take for you to hold firmly to your intention, your inspiring vision of being in relationship?

How might Mother Teresa inspire your heart's commitment to your intention?

    a. How could you have a generous heart toward others more often?

    b. What simple act of kindness is your heart asking you to offer to someone you love?

    c. What simple act of kindness is your heart asking you to offer to someone who is difficult for you to love?

    d. What would you have to believe so completely about your capacity to love that nothing could divert your attention?

    e. How might you expand your love?

Are you willing to allow your intention for peaceful relationships to transform you?

RESOLVE

As you are pondering happiness, how can you consider it in relationship to others?

How does attachment to the way you see create difficulty for you?

What are your thoughts on Dr. Warner's comment: *The world we respond to and our response to it are one*?

To improve our relationships, we have to develop honest "self-examination."

a. How might you be a problem for others?

b. How might you not be willing to see them and their concerns?

c. How are you not caring for the well-being of your relationships?

Honestly questioning yourself, with a sense of curious self-reflection, can reveal what has been hidden from sight.

It is good to pause here and wonder how much is happening in our own lives because of the energy we are projecting out into the world. Are we as innocent as we would like to believe? How does jumping to blame separate us from others?

Moments of peace and joy are already embedded in your heart. You have memories of wonderful encounters with friends.

a. What is your experience of the wonderful people you know?

b. How do you feel in their presence?

    c.   Even just thinking of them, what do you feel: appreciation, respect, compassion, or oneness?

    d.   In what ways do they light up your life?

    e.   Spend a few moments being grateful for having them as friends.

    f.   Can you feel your heart growing brighter?

Early in this book, you brought to mind many moments in your life that generate a joyful, loving heart. As you begin to consider one relationship, please revisit what makes you smile and dance, and the other heart-connecting activities. They appear in the Heart chapter and also in the Heart section of the Study Guide. Connect to that expansive energy. Let yourself bask in buoyant memories of friends and experiences in your life. Feel your heart expand, soften and let a smile arise.

Next, bring to mind one of your relationships that is troubled, but isn't too difficult for you to look at. Don't pick the most horrible, awful, no-good relationship. Freeing your heart in a less difficult struggle can give you confidence and leverage for the more entrenched ones.

Hold onto the receptive, loving energy that you've established. It is truly who you are and how you want to live your life. Own it completely as you begin to reflect on your heart-mind stance in this relationship. Take time to uncover genuineness. With gentleness, ask yourself:

    a.   What am I bringing to this relationship that I need to take responsibility for?

    b.   How am I part of the problem?

    c.   What am I clinging to?

    d.   How am I holding back?

e. How am I perhaps refusing to be helpful to the person?

f. Is this person really intending to be offensive? Even if they are, do I have to take offense?

g. What is their need?

h. What might be their struggle?

i. What is their heart inviting me to see?

j. What fuel have I thrown on their suffering?

k. What do people who love them see, that I am missing?

l. How might those faults I blame them for show up in me?

m. How does that keep me from seeing them or their good intent?

n. How would love respond? What is my heart whispering and needing me to hear?

o. What simple kindness does my heart want to offer?

p. How do I resolve to be with this person, as we go forward?

Remember what Mother Teresa said: *It is not what we do; it is how much love we put in the doing. It is not what we give; it is how much love we put in the giving.*

Since other people are always reflecting back to us what is unseen, what are you learning from your heart-mind mirror?

BREATHE

How often are you aware of breathing or holding your breath? How deeply and freely can you breathe? Do you allow your ribs to expand, top to bottom, side to side, front to back?

As you read the stories from our clients, what occurred to you? What did you think and feel?

How do these stories inspire you? How do they help you return to what your heart wants most?

Whose story reminded you of your life? What did you see that shifted your heart? How can you put that shift into action?

How might you step closer to one of the people in your life? What might you need to consider for the health of your relationship? ... and for the happiness you both desire?

Do you have more hope? What fresh possibilities are dawning on you?

What new thought or feeling have you had about who you can be in relationship?

TROUBLE

What gets in your way and prevents you from having the relationships you want?

Ask yourself these questions to see ways gossip and backbiting may be problematic for you:

a. Have you noticed yourself having a tendency to complain?

b. Where do you find yourself talking poorly about someone, drawing people into your web?

c. How compelling is it for you to join a tongue thrashing of someone?

d. Do you fear you'll be rejected if you don't join in?

e. What would it take for you to care enough about your own heart and others' hearts that you could become courageous and stop the injurious chitchat?

f. Freed from the need to gather baneful evidence, what might you see about the person or people you've been talking about?

g. How could you instead bond in love, caring and helpfulness?

What are the expectations or "shoulds" that serve as wedges in your relationships?

How can you be relaxed enough to be more comfortable with your own mistakes as well as others' mistakes?

Whom have you blamed for making you feel bad?

There is a common misperception that you are made to feel the way you do by something external. Consider instead the freeing conviction that you choose to feel the way you do. In the light of the freeing conviction, what familiar feelings do you need to consider more carefully?

How do feelings arise if they are not caused by someone else? Explore this question deeply.

What will help you take responsibility for your thoughts and feelings?

How can you ... *let the truth, especially the truth about the interior life of others, write itself upon your soul?*

Go back to the last study guide questions in Resolve and consider another friend as you answer those questions.

Reread Dr. Warner's quote: *To the degree that we become receptive and responsive to the truth, life will keep instructing us. It will teach us all sorts of fresh things about matters we thought we already understood. This is partly because we will no longer perceive them distortedly. We will be more open to seeing things as they are instead of anxiously twisting them to validate any lies we may be living.* What does this quote mean to you? How are you beginning to experience its truth?

What are you learning about you-in-relationship that is useful?

FREE

Think of a story – your own or one you've heard – that glows with heart-felt generosity.

There is nothing more potent or life-giving than merging the awareness of our heart-mind's state with action. It wakes up every cell of our body and ripples out and out into the world. Ponder these questions:

    a.   How might you be more present to people making requests of you?

    b.   How sensitive are you to the needs of others?

    c.   Are you practicing listening to your heart?

    d.   What will it take for you to follow its guidance?

    e.   What heartfelt action do you need to take today?

Choose one inspiring person in your life to consider in this moment.

    a.   What are their shining qualities?

    b.   What is it like to experience this person?

    c.   How does being with them increase who you are?

    d.   How would the people in your life benefit from knowing this person you've chosen?

    e.   How would the people in your life benefit from your being your best self?

Relationship requires that we show up as our best self. Who is your best self? What does he/she look like? act like? What would be the effect of your best self on other people?

Nasrudin was not known for having a humble heart. Yet he believed that no one was better at humility than he was. We can probably never learn humility at Nasrudin's feet. Except, maybe we are not so different from him and need to laugh at our own outrageousness. Consider these questions:

    a. What do you hold onto as your best or worst trait? How much pride or energy do you invest in your story?

    b. Are you continually measuring your worth or value against other people?

    c. How many times a day are you discourteous?

    d. How do you comment on others in small ways, even when it is only in your mind?

How does your communication uplift others?

What words or phrases might you consider eliminating from your vocabulary?

What kind or sacred words could you add?

With whom have you been compassionately silent? Who has been that for you? Who might need that?

What does it mean to warmheartedly listen to harsh, rude, intense, or critical words?

Ponder these questions about someone who has spoken to you without warmth:

a. What does the person really want to convey?

b. How much do you love? Is your heart so available that they know you are with them?

c. How can you provide safety that invites shades of tranquility to blossom in both hearts?

d. How can you show them you care?

e. Can you be so trustworthy that you can gently intervene?

f. Can your heart be so peaceful that you can say something difficult that needs to be said, in a way that can be heard?

Suppose for a moment you were going to participate in the Olympic event for happiness:

a. What would you have to study?

b. How much would you have to practice?

c. What would you have to let go of?

d. What kind of diet would you need to put yourself on?

e. What are the restrictions your trainer would enforce?

f. What vital self-talk would you have to commit to?

g. What would be your daily schedule?

h. Who would be on your support team?

No one has gotten to the Olympics by themselves or without effort.

Are there people you need to thank? Are there people you need to forgive? Whom do you need to ask for forgiveness? How can you speak bravely from your heart?

Exercise: Consciously fill your entire lungs with breath. Exhale slowly. This will begin to bring you into balance.

Please continue breathing deeply and slowly. Watch how deep, rhythmic breathing calms your mind and establishes you in your body, in the present moment.

Inhale deeply; exhale fully, each exhalation carrying away debris from your mind. Continue breathing with this awareness.

Taking your breath into a yet subtler dimension, imagine you are actually breathing into your heart, expanding it on each inhalation. As your heart becomes saturated with more breath, allow peaceful feelings to surface.

Experience your mind becoming more attuned to benevolence increasing in your heart ... each breath connecting you more to what really matters.

Breathing revitalizes you. Rest in peace and serenity. Breath is your life-line.

How much do you love? How can you be present to each and every person you meet in your day? How can you offer them your best?

REFERENCES

All of the poems in this book are written by Nancy Smyth. More can be seen in a form called "painted poetry" at www.nancysmythalchemist. com.

Nancy learned The Navajo chant while visiting Window Rock, Arizona.

Albom, Mitch. *Tuesdays with Morrie.* Random House, 1997.

The Arbinger Institute. *Leadership and Self-Deception.* Berrett-Koehler Publishers, Inc., 2000.

The Arbinger Institute. *Anatomy of Peace.* Berrett-Koehler Publishers, Inc., 2006.

Baha'i Sacred Writings. *Peace, More than an End To War.* Baha'i Publishing Trust, 1986.

Bahá'u'lláh. *Bahá'u'lláh's Teachings on Spiritual Reality.* Palabra Publications, 1996.

Buber, Martin. *I and Thou.* Reprint Continuum International Publishing Group, 2004.

Chambers, Edward. *Roots for Radicals.* The Continuum International Publishing Group Inc., 2006.

Chidvilasananda, Gurumayi. *Sadhana of the Heart.* SYDA Foundation, 2006.

Childre, Doc Lew, and Howard Martin. *The HeartMath Solution.* Harper Collins, 2000.

Chopra, Deepak MD, Menas Kafatos, Ph.D., Subhash Kak, Ph.D., Rudolph E. Tanzi, PhD., and Neil Theise, MD. *Can Brain Science Explain Experience?* HuffPost Healthy Living, May 5, 12, 19, 2014.

Dalai Lama, His Holiness and Howard C. Cutler, M.D. *The Art of Happiness.* Riverhead Books, 1998.

Duhigg, Charles. *The Power of Habit.* Random House, 2012.

Einstein Albert. *The Real Problem Is in the Hearts of Men.* New York Times, June 23, 1946.

Frankl, Viktor. *Man's Search for Meaning.* Simon & Schuster, 1959.

Gu, Master Mingtong. *Wisdom Healing.* Mingtong Gu, 2011.

Kahane, Adam. *Power and Love.* Berrett-Koehler Publishers, Inc., 2010.

Make-A-Wish® Arizona. *The Wishletter,* Edition 4: Summer 2014.

Muktananda, Swami. *From the Finite to the Infinite.* SYDA Foundation, 1994.

Nasrudin Stories

    Sorenen, Eric Kristen. *New Tales of Nasrudin.* Self, 2006.

    Shah, Indries. *The Exploits of the Incomparable Mulla Nasrudin.* E.P. Dutton & Co., Inc., 1972.

    http://www.harinam.com/nasrudin-tells-a-lie/

Nelson, Pete. *I Thought You Were Dead.* Workman Publishing Co., 2010.

Pearson, Carol Lynn. *The Lesson.* Gibbs Smith, Publisher, 1998.

Pflueger, Lynne and Michael Wenninger. *What Mary Says.* JSJ inc., 1997.

Scharmer, C. Otto. *Theory U: Leading from the Future as It Emerges.* Barret-Koehler Publishers, 2009.

Sardello, Robert and Cheryl Sanders-Sardello. *Silence: The Mystery of Wholeness.* Goldenstone Press, 2008.

Shantananda, Swami with Peggy Bendet. *Splendor of Recognition.* SYDA Foundation, 2003.

Stevens, Christina. *Love.* Hay House, Inc., 2014.

Twist, Lynne. *The Soul of Money: Reclaiming the Wealth of Our Inner Resources.* W.W. Norton & Company, 2003.

Ueland, Brenda. *Tell Me More.* Kore Press, 1998.

Warner, C. Terry. *Bonds That Make Us Free.* Shadow Mountain, 2001.

ABOUT THE

Sharon's energy has always been directed toward helping people live balanced, productive, joyful lives. She began her career by obtaining a master's degree in psychology. Sharon went on to be a therapist for many years and a healthcare executive for twenty years.

She leveraged the skills and experiences from those early roles to develop an executive coaching practice. As a Board Certified Coach, she continues to help leaders make meaningful contributions to their organizations and the world.

Since 2000 Sharon has written a monthly coaching blog, *Fresh Views.* Her essays are now collected in a book, *Fresh Views on Resilient Living.* Sharon also co-authored *Liberating Greatness, The Whole Brain Guide to an Extraordinary Life.*

Sharon's natural leadership skills, experiences, and innate abilities make her an ideal trainer for the Arbinger Institute. She currently co-leads the acclaimed master coaching program -- The Choice in Coaching.

Sharon has presented at many national conferences, and has been an invited guest on TV and radio shows.

Sharon has the presence of a wise woman wrapped in a spirit of lightness.

AUTHORS

In the mid 1980's, Nancy apprenticed with an Aztec Indian Medicine Man. Her apprenticeship was one of learning to see what is invisible to our physical eyes. She integrated this unique skill set into her coaching relationships. In 2006, Nancy received a Master Certified Coach credential through the International Coaching Federation.

Nancy's clients include Fortune 500 organizations, as well as smaller companies, couples, and individuals. Her focus guides clients to substantial lasting change, both personally and professionally. As coach, speaker, artist, and poet Nancy cultivates the experience, understanding, and expression of peace-filled solutions.

In 2003, The Arbinger Institute invited Nancy to co-develop and facilitate their training for coaches. This mastery-level program, The Choice in Coaching, continues to serve participants around the globe. She is also the course co-designer and facilitator for *The Anatomy of Peace,* Arbinger's most recent best seller. She serves as Arbinger's Director of Individual and Group Coaching and as an Executive Coach.

Nancy is an invited participant in Conversations Among Masters, SupporTED, Planetary Dance, and other collaborative projects.

Nancy's presence is delightfully tranquil while being powerfully transformative.

Made in the USA
Middletown, DE
08 November 2018